PENGUIN HANDBOOKS
PH 14
KEEPING POULTRY AND
RABBITS ON SCRAPS

Alan Thompson, author of the Poultry section of this book, kept poultry from the moment he left school. He obtained his technical knowledge at Harper Adams College and was Editor of *Poultry Farmer* for 15 years. He also farmed poultry at Courthouse Farm in Copthorne, Sussex, and his voice was familiar to all those who listened to the BBC's poultry talks.

Lafayette

Claude Goodchild, author of the Rabbit section of this book, spent the first 35 years of his life on an Essex farm and bred rabbits on a considerable scale from the age of 15. He went on

to run the largest rabbit farm of its time in England at Black Corner, near Crawley, Sussex. He started the Rex rabbit in England, was among the first to breed Chinchillas and visited many parts of the continent in an advisory capacity, including Russia at the invitation of the Soviet Government. He once fulfilled an order from the USA for 15,000 Chinchillas.

Photographia

Keeping Poultry

AND

Rabbits on Scraps

BY

ALAN THOMPSON

AND

CLAUDE H. GOODCHILD

*

PENGUIN BOOKS

HARMONDSWORTH · MIDDLESEX

PENGUIN BOOKS

Published by the Penguin Group

Penguin Books Ltd, 80 Strand, London WC2R ORL, England

Penguin Group (USA) Inc., 375 Hudson Street, New York, New York 10014, USA

Penguin Group (Canada), 90 Eglinton Avenue East, Suite 700, Toronto, Ontario, Canada M4P 2Y3
(a division of Pearson Penguin Canada Inc.)

Penguin Ireland, 25 St Stephen's Green, Dublin 2, Ireland (a division of Penguin Books Ltd)

Penguin Group (Australia), 250 Camberwell Road, Camberwell, Victoria 3124, Australia
(a division of Pearson Australia Group Pty Ltd)

Penguin Books India Pvt Ltd, 11 Community Centre, Panchsheel Park, New Delhi – 110 017, India

Penguin Group (NZ), 67 Apollo Drive, Rosedale, North Shore 0632, New Zealand
(a division of Pearson New Zealand Ltd)

Penguin Books (South Africa) (Pty) Ltd, 24 Sturdee Avenue,
Rosebank, Johannesburg 2196, South Africa

Penguin Books Ltd, Registered Offices: 80 Strand, London WC2R ORL, England

www.penguin.com

First published by Penguin Books 1941
This facsimile edition published 2008

1

All rights reserved

Printed in England by Clays Ltd, St Ives plc

ISBN: 978-0-141-03862-9

www.greenpenguin.co.uk

Penguin Books is committed to a sustainable future
for our business, our readers and our planet.
The book in your hands is made from paper
certified by the Forest Stewardship Council.

CONTENTS

INDEX TO POULTRY SECTION

INDEX TO RABBIT SECTION

EGGS FROM SCRAPS

By Alan Thompson

Editor *Poultry Farmer*

—

THE hen's egg is the finest concentrated food known to man. It is produced by a humble, and slightly ridiculous, creature whose remarkable qualities have never been justly appreciated.

A hen not only lays eggs: she grows corn and cabbages, onions and oats. As a Wiltshire farmer once observed – if my birds never laid another egg I would still keep them for their scratching and fertilising benefits to the soil.

Over a million people keep hens but few produce eggs with the utmost economy. Spacious grass range is not necessarily an advantage in this respect. Some of the best and most economical production is found in tiny city backyards.

The purpose of these pages, however, is to show how the maximum number of eggs can be obtained from the minimum amount of imported food. The hen will be introduced in a sober light with no attempt to extol its virtues at the expense of its weaknesses.

Let us first of all present the disadvantages of poultry keeping.

SNAGS IN POULTRY KEEPING

These can be summarised as follows: *Disease, time and expense.*

Unfortunately through indiscriminate breeding for very high production there are a number of strains which are either infected with disease or show little resistance to it.

Such birds are not only to be found in the hands of dealers at street and auction markets, but also on general farms.

Such stock can, however, easily be avoided if precautions are taken which are outlined later.

The time and labour involved are such as to be expected in the keeping of any livestock. The work of attending to poultry is relatively small, but it is constant. Unless the laying cage system is adopted the birds want food twice a day and cleaning out at least once a week. A hen is not a 'Hoover' which can be put away at week-ends.

As to the expense, this is dependent upon whether the poultry keeper is prepared to build or adapt his own appliances. If he is, the outlay can be negligible. But if not, as is more probable, the total expense of house and stock may vary between £7 and £20.

As compensation, it should, however, be pointed out that the owner has equipment which, with regular creosoting or tarring, will last him his lifetime – and few give up if they have once started with healthy stock. It is also reasonable to assume that the greater part, if not the whole, of the initial outlay will be paid for in the first year of lay out of profits from eggs over food.

This is without considering the benefits of a regular supply of new laid eggs and improved fertility of the garden.

THE START

Let us now consider how to start.

It would be proper to deal with equipment first, but let us take the hen before the house as she is the one vital factor in making a success of poultry keeping.

Although the beginner has the Domestic Poultry Keepers' Council placed at his disposal by the Government it is not in a position to supply stock.

It can, however, offer advice as to potential sources of supply.

So can the County Poultry Instructors, and the beginner

should not hesitate to consult the Poultry Press or the Experts on the trade papers, as he cannot take too much pains over the initial source of supply.

The Press, in fact, recognises this, for readers of the poultry and agricultural press are safeguarded from the dishonest dealer by the Poultry Advertisement Control Board which ensures that only suppliers of repute are allowed to advertise; and provides an Approval System by which the money for the purchase is not handed over to the seller until the goods have been received and, within 48 hours, approved.

The Board has also laid down the following definitions for various classes of stock and where the seller refuses to accept the Approval or Deposit System and is evasive in regard to the following definitions his offers should be treated with suspicion:

POULTRY AND FARM ADVERTISEMENT CONTROL BOARD REGULATIONS

CHICKS must be advertised as (1) 'Guaranteed not sexed'; (2) 'Sexed pullets'; (3) 'Sexed cockerels'; (4) 'Sex-linked pullets' or (5) 'Sex-linked cockerels.'

FEMALE POULTRY STOCK must be advertised as (1) PULLETS (birds up to 12 months old) and the month of hatching must be stated (e.g. 'September pullets'); (2) YEARLINGS (12 to 24 months) and both the month and year of hatching must be stated (e.g. 'May 1940 yearlings') or (3) HENS (over 24 months).

WHICH BREED?

The first and very natural question that every beginner asks is what breed should be kept?

The stereotyped answer is that there is no best breed: it

is a question of strain. You would not buy *any* Shorthorn if you wanted milk. You might get a beef type instead of a pedigree milker.

But in poultry, laying strains have been developed in some breeds more than others.

Thus the 'best' breed can be chosen from the following (in their order of their popularity at laying trials): *Rhode Island Reds, Light Sussex, Leghorns (Black, White, Brown), White Wyandottes, Buff Rocks*.

The *Rhode Island Red* has undoubtedly the largest number of pedigree breeders working upon it. It is the most popular and is the best all round layer – of brown or tinted eggs.

Rhode Island Red   Light Sussex

It is of a rich chestnut plumage colour, with yellow legs and orange eye (an important point to note in selecting pullets). It is a fairly good table bird but has rather a thin and prominent breast.

The *Light Sussex* on the other hand, which is a white bird with pretty black tickings on neck and a black tail, is a good table bird, a very good sitter (i.e. broods chicks) and is a very fair layer but is not so good a layer as the Rhode Island Red.

Its importance lies in the fact that it produces a splendid laying pullet when crossed with a Rhode Island Red male. This pullet can be identified at a day old by its plumage colour (see 'sex-linkage' later).

The *White Leghorn* is not only one of our finest layers, but being of a light weight and active disposition it is more suitable for intensive runs than Light Sussex.

Similarly the *Black Leghorn* is a magnificent layer of white eggs and is fully the equal of the Rhode Island Red in this respect, especially in city backyards where its great activity prevents it from laying on fat. Its carcase has, however, little meat when it comes to killing. It is a racy, jet black breed with a flop-over comb and a certain amount of flightiness.

The *Ancona* is a close relative of the Black Leghorn and differs chiefly in the fact that its black feathering is mottled or tipped with white.

The *Brown Leghorn* is another good laying 'light breed', originating from the Mediterranean and of a partridge colour.

The *Buff (Plymouth) Rock* is coloured as its name implies and is of heavier build. Its adherents esteem it for its vigour.

A breed of great popularity in the past, both for its eggs and meat, is the *White Wyandotte*, but it has lost ground owing to its low breeding fertility. Crossed, however, with the Rhode Island Red it is still one of our very best crosses.

The *Buff Orpington* is a variety that is still universally famous but it is handicapped by lack of breeders, and therefore fresh blood, and has a strong tendency to broodiness.

The *Barred Rock* is distinctive with its grey feathering barred with white and most of its laying strains originate from Canada where it is highly popular.

But it has never achieved the egg production in official laying tests over here of Rhode Island Reds, Leghorns and Sussex. Its value lies in the use that is made of it in developing the Cambridge auto-sexing breed, the Legbar, referred to later.

There are other breeds. Some of them are very beautiful and their development is a source of perpetual interest to the experienced breeder. But since eggs are the most important of our aims, we can ignore them.

Do not be misled, therefore, by the advice that Minorcas lay extra large eggs or that Welsummers or Langshans lay deep brown ones. It is true in some strains, but they are not foolproof.

If, however, the potential poultry keeper wants his stock to look handsome as well as productive, he has plenty of scope in either of the five pure breeds we have mentioned.

If, on the other hand, he would like to sacrifice uniformity in colour for a little extra vigour, he should choose a cross between any of the four breeds first mentioned.

Since most beginners like a decisive answer to the question: 'What breed shall I keep?' we would suggest to him the *Black Leghorn male crossed with R.I. Red hens.*

The pullets are black in colour with a little red ticking, so that they are suitable for smoky gardens. They are magnificent layers and, being very active, respond to close confinement.

When you kill them, after their year or two years of laying, they do not make such good 'boilers' as the Rhode Island Red crossed Light Sussex hen. But the latter has the disadvantage – or should it be advantage? – that it has a greater tendency to broodiness.

The Rhode × Sussex pullet is the most commonly kept, not only because of its larger body size and fine production but because the pullets can be identified on hatching by their down colour.

This is known as 'sex-linkage'.

SEX-LINKAGE

If you cross a 'gold' male, like Rhode Island Red, with a 'silver' hen, like Light Sussex, the male chicks take after the mother and are white or cream and the female chicks are reddish buff after their father.

This simple identification has made the cross universally popular and, in consequence, cheaper than the Black Leghorn × R.I. Red which, if you want all pullet chicks at a day old, needs the skilled vent examination of an expert – formerly a Japanese.

The Rhode Island Red cock × White Wyandotte hen is similarly sex-linked and the pullets are even better layers than the R.I. Red × Light Sussex. But it is not so common owing to the difficulty of getting good fertile strains of White Wyandottes.

Sex-linkage is not shown if the cross is made the other way round – that is, a 'silver' cock mated with 'gold' hens. But a Rhode Island Red male mated to the female progeny of a Light Sussex male crossed with Rhode Island Red hens shows sex-linkage.

Other examples of good sex-linked crosses are Brown Leghorn cocks × Light Sussex hens and the Legbar × Sussex.

The Legbar is an interesting innovation from the School of Agriculture at Cambridge. It is made from the Brown Leghorn and Canadian Barred Rock and has the peculiar

SEX LINKAGE

Gold Cock

Silver Hen

X

MATING OF PURE BREDS.

Silver Cockerel

Gold Pullet

CROSS-BRED PROGENY.

asset that it needs no outcross to distinguish the sex on hatching as there are marked differences in the male and female chick markings.

When it has been sufficiently bred and established it may become a very important variety, and it is already being used with great success in sex-linked crosses with Light Sussex.

WHAT AGE TO BUY?

The cheapest, and most instructive, way of starting poultry keeping is to buy sitting eggs.

The alternative, in the absence of more matured pullets at reasonable prices, is to buy day-old pullet chicks.

The *best* way, and the most foolproof, is to buy 3 month old pullets. 'Point of lay' pullets at 5 months are the most immediately responsive to results, but under war food rationing were seldom available. In any case 'point of lay' is a most misleading term when used by the dealer.

Of other variants, it is possible to buy 4 to 8 week old pullets, and since the latter are fully weaned and cooled off from the brooder they are extremely popular.

The purchase of 'yearlings', that is, layers between the ages of 12–24 months, is sometimes also profitable, particularly in early spring when a certain number of eggs can still be expected from them, and when they cease to lay they can be eaten or used as broodies.

The danger exists that yearlings may be unsound, especially if bought at markets, and it is obvious that no producer wishes to dispose of yearlings in the peak of production except for some special reason.

To give some idea of the costs of the different systems, we give the *lowest* price we would advise paying for a good commercial pullet at various ages: Day old, 1/6; 4 weeks, 3/–; 8 weeks, 6/–; 3 months, 10/–.

It is possible to buy cheaper chicks than these, especially in markets. But it must not be forgotten that an extra shilling is quickly made up by a good layer. It only means three or four eggs. Cheap chicks are not worth the risk and it is better if in doubt to pay a good deal more.

One shilling for each week of the chick's age provides a reasonable basis for assessing the retail price.

WHAT TIME TO BUY

The best hatching date for a pullet is between mid-March and mid-April. She will then start laying in September–October and, if well managed, carry on until the late summer of the following year.

If she is hatched in January or February there is a risk that she may moult in the same year that she has been hatched. If she is hatched in May or later she will be slightly longer in attaining maturity or starting to lay. She may take eight months instead of five to seven months. This is, perhaps, because she misses that spring flush of grass and insect life.

Pre-war it was the practice of the commercial breeder to concentrate on March as his chief hatching month and November as his second string. With the November chick he avoided the spring 'glut' when egg prices fell heavily and the pullets maintained the flock output when the spring-hatched layers were falling off.

But in war egg prices are more static and it is of little concern to the beginner when his chicks are hatched, except that in late summer they take longer to mature, and there is the risk with the autumn-hatched chicks that the cod liver oil which is needed to reinforce winter sunlight may not be of sufficiently high quality.

If, however, the beginner is bent on maintaining a steady output throughout the year, and thus saving the need of preserving any eggs, March and September are the two hatching months to choose.

HOW MANY EGGS TO EXPECT

The accepted production of a normal pullet in her first twelve months of laying is 150 eggs.

But kept in small units, where care is taken in the selection of the stock and in seeing that every bird has its fair share of the mash trough and broodiness is promptly checked, a first year average of 200 eggs per bird is by no means uncommon.

If we assume, however, that an April-hatched pullet lays 165 eggs, this is how we might expect her to lay them:

October	..	8	April ..	..	20
November	..	10	May ..	..	19
December	..	12	June ..	..	16
January	..	13	July ..	..	14
February	..	15	August..	..	12
March ..	..	18	September	..	8

TOTAL .. 165

It will be noticed from this that the zenith of production is in April.

In well-managed units, a larger output will be obtained from October to December; this is dependent on early hatching, good rearing and good housing.

If the paper figure for a pullet's production is given as 150 then that for hens in their second year of lay (i.e. yearlings) will be 125. Pre-war it was customary to replace 75 per cent of the stock yearly and only keep on 25 per cent of the hens.

The small poultry keeper is in the fortunate position of being able to observe his stock closely and so make a more definite decision on the knotty problem of which pullets to keep on, over a two or three months' moult-rest.

HOUSING

We have now discussed the type of stock to buy, the age to buy it, and the cost and probable output.

Logically we should now give information upon the methods of rearing and managing those birds. But the next point to decide is the type of house the layers will eventually live in. This is because the system of rearing depends upon the laying house which in any case must be ordered or built well in advance.

THE LAYING HOUSE

There are only two essentials in a house for layers.

One is the largest quantity of air without draughts; and the other is a dry floor – a feature which is much more closely related to ventilation than to weather conditions or to outside moisture.

A fowl sweats through its beak and the air in a badly ventilated house overcrowded by birds becomes saturated with moisture. This is absorbed by the litter which remains damp and becomes a ready medium for disease bacteria and worms.

A hen can tolerate extreme cold but it has a great aversion to draughts and cold winds and to getting its feet wet.

Thus we have known birds to winter in apple trees in perfect bloom but to catch colds in elaborate houses.

But this is no argument in favour of the orange box type of house which the beginner is frequently advised is good enough for his birds.

There is, for example, a very popular small house of 6 ft. long by 4 ft. wide. It is admirable for rearing pullets, and indeed will suffice for layers on extensive range. But it is futile where birds are kept under very cramped conditions and need exercise in dry litter.

The object of housing is to maintain the birds in comfort and cleanliness so that the food given is not used solely for maintenance but for eggs. Protection from vermin and humans, and the control of the ground are further reasons.

There are many types of house, but they can be divided into three general classes; *intensive*, that is, where birds are kept completely under cover; *semi-intensive* where the house may not be large enough to keep the birds all the time under cover and it has outside runs attached; and *extensive*, on free range where the house is relatively small and portable, and, owing to a floor of slatted pieces of wood or perches over wire netting instead of a solid floor, the birds do not make use of it during the day time.

The *Sussex Ark* or Night Ark is a good example of the last type and the movable *fold pen* is an adaption from this.

INTENSIVE HOUSES

Let us first deal with the type of house suitable for the man with very little space, who is obliged to keep his birds under very *intensive* conditions.

Obviously an outside run is impractical because, since alternate runs could not be provided (as we shall presently emphasise), it would soon become a quagmire and caked with manure.

The small, dog-kennel type of house with a small, permanent run is not only an eyesore to the countryside but a centre of disease.

If there is a small area of grass it would be much better employed rearing chicks or dug up and growing cabbages.

The intensive house must therefore provide each bird with adequate scratching space to keep it occupied – and not poking its beak into the rump feathers of its neighbours throughout the day.

In our view the amount of floor space per bird should not be less than 6 sq. ft. and could be considerably more.

Thus a house 8 ft. long by 6 ft. deep would hold eight pullets. This is the general principle. In practice manufacturer's dimensions vary considerably, as also the designs.

When in doubt always order the larger house.

In some houses the roosting section is separated from the scratching by a partition. In others the perches are all part of the same house as it is more economical in space.

Many keen backyarders add extra scratching sections, or wire sun-porches or even exercising runs underneath the house.

The covered run extension is a most desirable addition.

The front of the scratching section can consist of wire-netting or trellis except for 2 ft. of weather boarding at floor level and an adjustable hood protecting against driving rain if desired. The roof can be built of felt or corrugated iron, over wood. The scratching shed extension may be cheaply made of any materials, providing it is a dry playground for the birds. It can be added to any house.

A particular advantage of such an extension is that it provides temporary accommodation for growing pullets, with a low perch at the back, when the house proper is occupied by adults.

Houses are made with span roofs, two-thirds span or lean-to, the slope being either to the front or to the back.

The best types for ventilation are span or two-thirds span and a good example of the former is the 'Lancashire Cabin'.

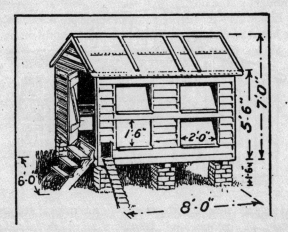

This resembles a large tool shed with windows on either side. It has plenty of *head room* which is essential for ventilation and is a point worth considering with a tall owner. The house is also excellent for permanent sites in exposed or wet areas.

But it has the disadvantage that unless protected side openings are made it does not admit direct sunlight.

Direct sunlight is very greatly desired – especially under intensive conditions – as otherwise it must be replaced with cod liver oil which may not be of high quality in wartime.

Hence the front of the house in the lean-to types is worth

considering. As much of the direct rays should be admitted as possible without driving rain to wet the litter. This is best effected by providing an adjustable weatherboard hood, as illustrated below.

In one design (see photographs and sketch) the wire netting is projected outwards as a protection against bad weather and this netting should not exceed ¾ inch mesh (if obtainable!) to keep out sparrows.

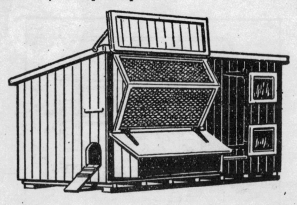

Obviously the house should face southerly where possible and if it has no floor the surface water should be carried away by outside trenches and the foundation well raised and tamped down with cinders or brick rubble.

If the house has a floor it should be raised on bricks at least a foot from the ground, as the litter keeps drier and there is no cover for rats.

The perches are usually arranged along the back wall or at one end and should be out of direct draughts but at the same time should receive plenty of air.

There should be no suspicion of 'fug' when you come to attend to the occupants in the early morning.

Eight inches of perch space should be allowed per bird and the perches should be 2 ft. 6 in. to 3 ft. from the ground,

2 ft. (minimum) from the eaves with a sliding out droppings tray of metal or matchboard 6 in. beneath them.

A good perch is 3 in. wide, 2 in. deep, with a bevelled edge, placed 10 in. from the back wall and 14 in. from the next perch. It should not be permanently fixed as the ends would offer a harbourage for redmite.

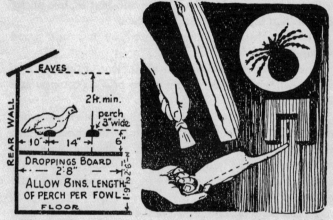

The perch sockets could in fact be made of metal angle irons or even stout screws or nails. It would be then easy to spray the ends with a mixture of paraffin and creosote at six-monthly intervals.

The *nests* can be placed inside, against the wall in the darkest corner of the house; or outside, that is framed into the front or the side of the house projecting outwards with a flap lid for collection. If put inside the house they should be raised off the ground to give the maximum scratching space, and to keep the litter out a low litter flap can also be fitted.

They should not, however, be raised to the same level as the roosts or put near them, as otherwise birds have an unpleasant habit of sleeping on top or inside and messing the nest litter.

Such habits should, incidentally, be checked at once, as once formed they are difficult to stop.

Pre-war nest boxes were made of orange boxes as the partitions were of the right size: 12 to 14 in. square, and any boxes of this size will do. Some poultry keepers use colony nests of say 2 ft. 6 in. long by 14 in. deep.

One nest for four pullets is quite sufficient as, like ducks, they will all lay in one nest if they can.

The best litter is straw followed by hay and wood shavings.

The last is not so satisfactory if the floor of the nest is of wire mesh, which some people use to provide coolness and less cover for fleas.

Most light is needed in front of the house but small *windows* lighting the floor should be fitted low down on each side and under the droppings board. If they can slide open so much the better in hot weather. Baffled air inlets should also be arranged near floor levels (not over the perches) and outlets in the ridge.

To complete the equipment of the house, a V-shaped *wet mash trough* raised on legs 6 in. off the floor is required. It need not have closed ends but it should be long – 4 ft. for ten birds, as the practice of feeding in old kettles and bowls is most reprehensible.

There are a number of good *water buckets* and fountains on the market but the best type is undoubtedly a small bucket placed loosely in a slotted platform attached to the side wall with a shallow pan beneath to keep drips out of the litter. The important point is that the water must be kept away from the litter which will otherwise be scratched into it by active hens.

A grit box with partitions for [flint or gravel grit and cockle shell or limestone grit can be hooked to the side wall.

If the beginner wants to complete the job he will make a

greenfood rack like a miniature hay crib also to hang from the wall.

One other indispensable piece of equipment in an intensive house or indeed in any house (including a fold where the owner does not want potholes in his ground) is a *dust bath*.

This is nature's remedy for getting rid of insects. What is required is a large box of dry earth, ashes or sand sprinkled with flowers of sulphur. It is best placed in a corner of the

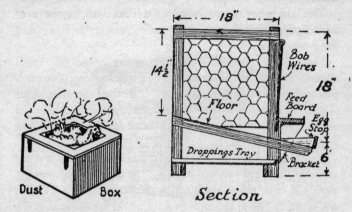

scratching annexe to prevent dust and if a lip is nailed on all round this will also prevent the dust from being scattered.

A few nails on a board for carrying split swedes and turnips are another useful little extra.

Floor litter is the remaining and rather troublesome item. Wheat straw with an under covering of peat moss is the ideal scratching material. Peat moss is excellent because it is very absorbent, lasts for a long time and afterwards forms perfect compost for the garden.

But those who wish to use cheaper materials have the following alternatives: straw chop, wood shavings, sawdust, leaves, dry earth, ashes.

There should be at least 4 in. and it should be changed when it becomes damp or smells.

An off-shoot from the intensive house is the *laying battery* or *cages* in which layers are confined in a wire netting or metal cage of some 14 in. by 18 in.

The system sounds cruel to those who do not know how extremely well pullets lay in it or how they appreciate and respond to individual feeding and a clean floor.

There is little risk of one of the dangers of intensive poultry keeping – feather or egg eating, and laying cages provide the very great advantage that bad layers are immediately spotted.

One of the weaknesses of the beginner is that he invariably hangs on to birds which are not economic to keep.

The disadvantage of the battery, although it can hardly be described as such, is that daily and not occasional cleaning is essential (except perhaps in outdoor cages) and a strong type of pullet is required as there are some breakdowns if the diet is over-stimulating or consists of too much wet swill.

On the other hand it is the one system where the owner can go away for the week-end knowing that the birds will have enough food and water till he comes back and that the eggs will be waiting for him, having gently rolled down the sloping wire tray on which the birds stand, to the egg rack in front.

There are two systems of laying cage management; one indoors, the other out.

The indoor system is the most popular as the birds can be attended to in carpet slippers and sparrows can be kept out. But the outside system takes less space. Six pullets can be accommodated in a space of 8 ft. by 3 ft. And there is smaller initial outlay as only the cages are required with a weather hood and no house in addition.

The single or double metal dropping trays in the inside battery need cleaning daily. But with outside cages the droppings can be left longer. This is no advantage, however, if they become a manure heap surrounded by a rich growth of stinging nettles.

Semi-intensive housing systems can, of course, adopt the same types of house as for intensive with the advantage that there are outside runs, or to be exact, two or four runs. For no poultry keeper should plan just one outside run. However small each one is, he must provide sufficient netting or trellising for two runs.

The reason is that if the runs are used alternately at say one-month or three-month intervals, it not only gives a chance for a succulent grass sward to be established but it is better for the health of the birds.

The droppings are given a chance to dissolve, especially if aided by sweeping up and raking, by frequent dressings of ground lime, either slaked or unslaked, which should be put on even before the birds have access to the runs.

Lime, however, does not kill any infectious bacteria, so if the poultry keeper has the space and the capital he will make an even better job of his poultry outfit if he provides *four* runs and crops, or grasses down one or two of them.

As shown later on under 'disease', it is the digging and resting of the ground which is the best control against worms and tuberculosis.

In sheltered spots, such as, for example, Surrey birch-woods, it is possible to use a low *laying ark* which is widely used for commercial rearing.

The nest boxes are either attached or placed against the windward side. No cover is of course provided by the house in bad weather but the initial cost is small.

There is one other type of house in which no fencing is required and is suitable where there is a large area of flat lawn. It is known as the *fold pen*.

Like the ark it is a low squat apex type of house with a wire netting extension.

The secret of it is to move it daily so that the birds get a fresh piece of grass to scratch over. It is moved either by wheels or by a lever which swings it sideways.

Its chief advantages are that it is comparatively cheap, it provides complete control of the ground and therefore the health of the birds, and no wire netting is required.

Its disadvantage is that a fresh area of grass must be found for it daily, otherwise the birds do not get their ration of fresh grass and tend to grub out potholes.

There is also an occasional tendency, where the birds were not reared in folds, to feather-peck and egg-eat.

The design of the nest box is thus important.

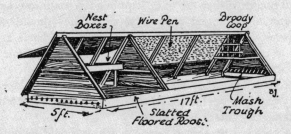

It should be placed on the opposite side to the pophole entrance to the roosting section; and three-ply hinged flaps with circular entrance holes to the nest boxes prevent the birds roosting in them or taking an unhealthy interest in the eggs.

A good size of fold for up to 20 pullets is 18 ft. long, 5 ft. wide and 5 ft. high with 5 ft. by 4 ft. roosting section.

Such a fold can be moved sideways one end at a time and the birds soon get used to it. It is best to start at one end of the lawn and work up and down leaving strips for the return journey. The droppings under the slats should be shovelled up after moving and stored or put on the garden.

For 12 pullets a fold 11 ft. long and 5 ft. wide would be sufficient. 7 ft. 7 in. of the fold could form the run section and it could be lifted by handles at each end.

There is a good deal to be said for a smaller fold still, so that it can be easily moved by ladies and can occupy odd corners which are inaccessible to larger designs.

The National Utility Poultry Society, 4 Arne Street, London, WC2, for example, issues a free design of a fold for 6 pullets with full instructions upon how to make it.

This fold is 6 ft. by 4 ft. and the roosting section is covered with felt. It is so light that it can easily be moved over sections of the kitchen garden not in use, and if 12 birds are kept, two folds of this size will be more easily manipulated than one larger one.

All houses, if they are to be kept in good condition, need an annual creosoting or even tarring. They should not, however, be creosoted if the birds are in residence as it should be allowed to dry for ten days before they come in contact with it.

Creosote has a most salutary effect on insect pests, especially when (pre-war) it was diluted with paraffin, but it tends to darken the interior of a house.

So here is a lime-wash recipe which, it should be noted, has no lethal effect on one particularly tiresome little insect, the redmite, whose habit is to make onslaughts on the roosting birds at night, and retire to crevices in the day.

Paraffin or creosote sprayed into the corners is the best remedy for them.

LIME-WASH RECIPE

Slake half a bushel of fresh lime with water, in tub; retain steam by placing sacks over.

Strain liquid through fine strainer to remove all coarse particles and mix with a peck of salt dissolved in warm water. Add also 3 lb. of thin glue, grease or size boiled to a thin paste. Add 5 gallons of clean water to the mixture, stir well. Allow to stand for a day or two and then apply hot. One pint will cover a square yard.

RUNS AND FENCING

A good average height for wire netting is 5 ft. with a 'trip' wire if necessary fixed six inches above the top selvedge. The best gauge, is 17 or 18, 19 being too fine, and it is sometimes considered an advantage to buy in two strips, the bottom 2 ft. of 2-inch mesh, and the top 3 ft. of 3-inch mesh.

The object of this is that the lower half rots first and is more easily cut by scythes. But in actual fact the posts, unless pressure creosoted, are likely to go before the netting. Ten feet is a good distance apart for them and they can, of course, be made of old iron rods or any blitzed junk that can be found.

One poultry keeper uses cuttings from the sallow willow as they take root instead of rotting and provide shade. But they grow and shoot very rapidly when once they take hold.

Other suggestions for shade and ornament are rose climbers and cultivated blackberries which can be trained over the netting.

Since wire netting requires a permit from the County Agricultural Executive Committee to obtain (unless Area

Organisers can secure a release), the alternatives are trellising made from plaster lathes or junk wood and string netting, or the protection provided by hedges like privet reinforced with boarding or corrugated iron at the foot.

One bundle (500 ft.) of 4 ft. plaster lathes will make a lattice trellis which will extend to 3 ft. long by 2 ft. 4 in. high.

GRASS RUN MANAGEMENT

Normal stocking on grass pens where space is available is 20 to 25 sq. yds. per bird. This area is usually too extravagant for most suburban gardens, but can be reduced to as low as 8 sq. yds. per bird if special attention is given to the turf, *and there are alternative runs.*

Where grass exists it is well worth preserving, as good grass goes a long way to preserve health of birds, to provide nutriment and to clean the ground. Proceed as follows, when establishing a pen on rough grass:

Mow off long, coarse growth. Dress lightly with lime. Turn in birds and let them scratch out weeds and matted bottoms. Roll well with heavy hand roller. Cut out obvious weed patches and bare spots. Fill in with fresh sods of odd pieces of turf and grass weeded from garden. Firm patches by patting down with flat of spade. Cover these spots with thorn or wire netting to keep off birds till the turf knits.

Grass seed may be sown if no turf is available. Thereafter treat as a lawn. Mow with lawn mower set high, and regularly roll during months when grass is growing. Mowing will kill practically all useless weeds, and in second year fine grass and clover will predominate.

Mowing encourages fresh growth, which absorbs droppings, and is keenly relished by fowls. General scratching does not permanently damage vigorous short grass.

If grass will not grow, dig over at intervals, remove top layer when heavily caked with manure, and sweep off droppings in dry weather.

FEEDING THE LAYER

Pre-war, a layer's rations consisted of 2 oz. of corn and 2½ oz. of layer's mash a day. Thus six pullets needed nearly 12 lb. of food a week.

The mash was fed either morning or evening, and given dry or mixed with water or housescraps to a crumbly consistency.

The mash was fed in long troughs, not on the ground, or in small bowls, so that every bird could get a fair share, allowing 6 in. of trough per bird.

The corn was given in one feed, or divided into two feeds, the smaller feed being scattered in scratching litter to promote exercise.

In addition, the layers were given fresh greenstuff and clean water *ad lib.*, and two kinds of grit – (*a*) flint grit or gravel; (*b*) cockleshell or limestone grit.

Under post-war conditions poultry keepers with not over 25 birds receive only just over 2 oz. of Balancer meal (laying mash) daily per bird and no corn on the surrender (at some periods) of egg registrations.

This Balancer meal is obtained by filling in a registration card obtainable from the local Food Office and sending it to Ministry of Agriculture, Lytham St. Annes, Lancs., stating the number of birds under 13 (chicks being counted as adults) and the date when they were purchased.

But 2 oz. of Balancer meal per day is not sufficient for a layer as indicated from the pre-war ration above and would only suffice for a 10-week old pullet.

A PULLET'S COMPLETE DAILY RATION

This 2 oz. represents one small teacup. With it must be mixed about 8 oz. of minced kitchen scraps, potatoes and vegetables. This is the equivalent of a ½-pint glass and with the tea-cup of meal forms a laying hen's complete daily ration.

This meal-and-scraps mash can be fed to the birds two or three times daily in roomy troughs.

The largest feed should be the last, a good hour before roosting so that they have plenty of time to fill their crops.

In addition they should be given all the *fresh green food* – cabbage or sprout leaves, split swedes, lettuce, that can be spared and they will consume, and it should be racked or hung up off the ground.

HOUSE SCRAPS

BALANCER MEAL

Small Tea-Cup

½ Pint Glass

SUBSTITUTES FOR CORN

The first feed of the day should not be so large that the birds remain lethargic afterwards. In pre-war days this was achieved by giving a light scratch feed or corn.

Many poultry keepers consider that their birds will not lay without corn but in actual fact it is the mash – and particularly the meat or fish meal in the mash – which produces eggs. But grain had undoubted advantages, especially as an exerciser.

Sunflowers and *Maize* are useful alternatives for those with the ground available.

Of these an early ripening Canadian maize such as Jehu offers the greatest possibilities.

Although corn is not essential, some poultry keepers provide an imitation corn with large baked crumbs from stale bread, pieces of bacon rind and limestone grit. Or they make a paste of laying meal and cooked and finely minced scraps, put through the mincer to form pellets and then baked in the oven.

A word must also be said for the *acorn*. A hen will not be attracted by a *whole* acorn and a prejudice exists against feeding it because of the risk of olive-coloured or black yolks – as has undoubtedly occurred with ducks.

But there is little evidence in support of this with poultry and, in any case, the poultry keeper consuming all his own eggs will be prepared to run this risk if he can obtain such a cheap and valuable food.

If the acorns are roughly broken or crushed, the hens will readily eat them whether fed green or much weathered.

They pick out the kernel, leaving the shell (which may cause the discoloured yolks) and they can be given a good handful per bird daily.

It is best to dry the acorns for six weeks, spread on mesh netting or sacks in a shed, as they can then be stored.

They can also be ground into meal.

Similarly *beechmast*, introduced gradually, makes an excellent feed, especially if shelled, as the kernels of the beech-nut are very rich in protein.

But little is known about *horse chestnuts*, although they are considered too bitter and binding for pigs.

There can be no harm in feeding them in small quantities if they are soaked, skinned and boiled. But who has the time?

SUPPLEMENTS FOR BALANCER MEAL

The most easily obtainable supplement for bulking the Balancer meal is the *potato*, either whole or as peel. A bird will easily eat 4 or 5 oz. of potatoes a day and they can form over 50 per cent of the mash.

The potatoes should be steamed – the water poured off – and mashed up. A special potato masher has been devised for quantities.

The sprouts should be rubbed off late in the season and no green potatoes should be included.

The second best home-provided food is fish waste and stale bread, and finally dried *grass mowings*.

These mowings should not be more than 3 in. long and should be dried quickly to preserve their green colour by spreading out very thinly immediately after cutting. Drying needs a big area, such as a concrete garage floor, or thin hessian on netting raised off the ground. In hot sun, if turned over two or three times daily, it will dry in two days and can be stored packed lightly in sacks.

Dried grass does not mix well with the wet kitchen scraps and meal, but if the birds are hungry they will eat it and it will not only prove a valuable food but will keep the yolk colour a rich yellow in winter.

Any stale *bread*, not fit for human consumption, can just be soaked and included in the mash as it is.

If the time can be spared it should be baked like a rusk in the oven and then exploded through a kitchen mincer. It will make a floury meal of several grades and can be stored in a tin and used to dry off the meal.

PREPARING HOUSE SCRAPS

As a rule it is preferable to mince raw vegetables rather than cook them or at least to mince them before cooking, and an electric mincer, the Proctor, has been specially designed by Major Products, of Chesterfield, for this purpose.

So failing raw mincing, or mincing before cooking, all cabbage leaves, potato peel, meat scraps can be simply steamed or boiled in a pot or simmered in an oven (or hay box); chopped up; and the Balancer meal ration mixed in to form a crumbly meal.

Whilst it is best not to have the food too sloppy, it is sometimes difficult to dry off without exceeding the meal ration. But it would be a pity to lose the valuable minerals in the

CUSHION OF HAY
TO GO OVER PAN

PAN FOR
MASH

LINING OF
BROWN PAPER

THICK LAYER
OF HAY ON
BOTTOM

CLOSED CAN BE
USED AS SEAT

cabbage water and rather than strain it off it can be given in the drinking water.

The ideal consistency for the mash is, however, a soft ball which will break up into fragments when put in the troughs.

The old-fashioned *hay box* is an excellent way of cooking scraps.

It consists of a box lined with paper and hay in which the pot is put, after half an hour's boiling and covered with a cushion and lid.

If put in overnight it will be ready by the morning.

It will not, however, soften bones and particularly the small bones from fish heads and filletings. This *fish waste* is still available in some areas and forms the most important productive material in a layer's mash.

The value of an egg lies in its protein content and its vitamin D and minerals. Protein is found in meat and fish scraps, blood, skim milk. Fish is perhaps the most useful as it also contains phosphates and salt.

If any quantity can be obtained this is best dealt with in a pressure cooker of the domestic 'Pentecon' type. This cooker reduces the fish bones to a pulpy mass of great succulence to hens and ducks.

Failing a pressure cooker, bring the fish waste to the boil, just covered by water, simmer for 10 minutes, cool, and put through a kitchen mincer.

Although in peacetime not more than 10 per cent of fish meal was recommended in a mash, considerably more *fresh* fish waste could be included with no unsatisfactory results whatever.

In the absence of fish, which may, in any case, be included in the Balancer meal, a pinch (only) of salt and a table-spoonful of limestone flour can be added to the final mixing.

The only food materials which should not be given to hens are rhubarb and tea leaves and certain wild seeds and shrubs, such as yew and laburnum, mentioned in the Disease chapter later.

There is no harm in small quantities of dropped fruit and fruit peel of apples and plums. Although carrot tops and pea pods are fibrous and difficult to use, they will be eaten if chopped up fine.

The carrot, although good for hens and especially for chicks when minced raw, is not so popular with them as the potato and artichoke.

One of the most valuable vegetable proteins for hens is afforded by the pea and the bean (haricot, runner and french). They are best dried and minced.

Here is a list of the foods the poultry keeper can grow for his birds:

Artichoke, Jerusalem	Carrots	Mangolds
Beans: Broad, Dwarf, Haricot and Runner	Kale (Thousand-headed and Rape)	Onions
Buckwheat	Leeks	Peas
Beet	Lettuce (summer)	Potatoes
Broccoli, Sprouting	Lucerne	Spinach
Brussels Sprouts	Linseed	Sunflower
Cabbage: Spring, Winter and Savoy	Maize	Swedes
		Turnips

GROW YOUR OWN POULTRY FOOD?

What should a small flock owner grow on half an acre to supplement his poultry rations?

Most productive crop is the potato. It is also the most reliable and the easiest to harvest.

But the potato is not the simplest to feed. Grain is easiest to feed because, apart from threshing, it requires no preparation like cooking and mincing. Best grain is either wheat or maize.

Maize (of quick growing Canadian or Golden Standard strains) is the least complicated to harvest because the birds will clean the cobs themselves. But it is not as easy to grow as wheat, because it is a slow starter and in May is subject to attack by birds and vermin. These attacks are not so severe if the acreage sown is larger.

Of spring wheats, Atle, sown not later than March, may yield half a ton of wheat from a half acre if the ground is in good heart – that is, sufficient to supply half the food ration for 20 birds for a year. But this is contingent upon no depredations, particularly from sparrows, and upon cutting and binding by an adjoining friendly farmer.

Thrashing must be secured through the same source as it otherwise presents difficulties, unless the sheaves are thrown to the birds for them to pick the heads and use the straw as litter.

Most wheat yields from half an acre in a suburban area, isolated from other grain crops, would probably not exceed 5 cwts. – sufficient for a yearly half day's ration for ten pullets.

This compares with 4 tons of potatoes (which is the equivalent of 1 ton of grain).

And since most smallholders cannot get their ground prepared and sown by March or even by the first fortnight in April, potatoes and maize have obvious advantages.

HATCHING

The best way for a beginner to start is to buy 3 months'
old pullets or, failing that, day old or eight weeks old pullet
chicks as previously indicated.

But readers who are interested and have a Domestic
Poultry-keepers' Council expert to help them will derive
interest from hatching their own eggs.

The advantage is that the initial cost is lower and you
can ensure that the ensuing pullets are hatched from good
sized and textured eggs.

The disadvantage is that it is seldom that broody hens
are available in the early spring months, such as March,
when you wish to hatch the eggs.

Broody hens are also fickle and sometimes inclined to
desert; and to obtain eight good pullets it would be
necessary to sit at least two sittings. This is because the
average number of chicks hatched from a sitting of 12 eggs
is 8, and half will be cockerels.

Incubators, reliable as the good makes are, are obviously
uneconomic for such small numbers and will not be considered in this book. Helpful information is, however,
readily available in regard to them and beginners are
cautioned against cheap makes and second-hand incubators.

The normal way of buying a sitting is '12 eggs and
infertiles replaced' or '15 eggs and infertiles not replaced'.

An infertile is an egg whose white germ cell (noticeable
on the yolk surface of a raw egg) has not received the sperm
of the cock. It remains 'clear' during incubation and can in
fact be eaten.

It is for the reader to decide whether he chooses 12 eggs
and infertiles replaced, or 15.

Personally we should choose the 15 because if we purchased two sittings this would mean 30 eggs.

Since an average hen cannot comfortably take more than
13 eggs (and tends to break any over this number) it would

be necessary to divide these 30 eggs over 3 hens, giving 10 to each, and it is an additional insurance against one broody 'packing up'.

If, however, 12 are purchased, it certainly provides a precaution against an unlucky break of infertiles, but it is a nuisance returning them (as the breeder has the right to demand) and also it would mean a further lot of late hatched chicks.

This would prove particularly tiresome in a confined space as the two broods could not be amalgamated.

The weight of a hatching egg should be at least $2\frac{1}{8}$ oz., but there is no advantage in an egg over $2\frac{1}{2}$ oz. as there are difficulties in hatching such large eggs.

The shell should be a perfect oval with no rings or blemishes especially towards the narrow end. The shell should be fine textured and with a certain gloss, although a high polish is easily obtained by artificial means.

Naturally if the poultry keeper has a preference for eating brown shelled eggs this is one way of making reasonably certain of getting them.

But the brown pigment soon fades in a heavy layer and exceptionally deep brown eggs such as are found in some strains of Welsummers, Croad Langshans and Marans are usually laid by pullets which take long rests in between.

It should also be added that brown shells contain no more nourishing contents than white shells, which are the fashion in America.

The price of the sitting obviously depends upon the pedigree of the stock. We should expect good pullets by paying not less than 1/– an egg.

SITTING THE HEN

The nesting boxes can be placed anywhere either in the open or in a shed. But steps must be taken to see that the hens cannot escape when taken off for their daily feed, as few are well trained enough to go back to their nest box on request.

The box should be about 14 to 16 in. square and have a wire mesh floor and a solid front as a protection against rats.

Now it is a debatable point as to whether a sod of turf should be put in the bottom of the coop or not, as good

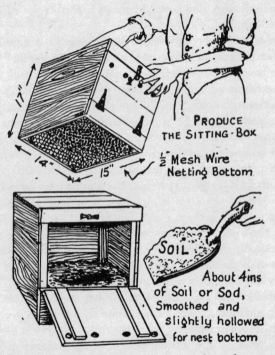

PRODUCE THE SITTING-BOX

$\frac{1}{2}$" Mesh Wire Netting Bottom

SOIL

About 4 ins of Soil or Sod, Smoothed and slightly hollowed for nest bottom

chicks are hatched without it. But it can do no harm and it prevents any risk of lack of moisture. It also approaches the natural conditions of the 'stolen' nest in the hedgerow.

So cut a piece of turf of the same dimensions as the floor of the coop. Cut off a saucer-shaped piece of soil from the centre of the turf so as to make a depression, and place it in the box grass side upwards.

Push it well into the corners so that no egg can roll *out* into them and be irretrievable by the hen's beak.

On the top of the turf mould a little straw or hay into the form of a nest and dust with insect powder or derris.

Put in a couple of china or 'pot' eggs, or unfertile fresh eggs.

Then dust your broody hen with insect powder and shut her in the box.

Next day, at the same time that you will in future feed her, take her off for 20 minutes for a meal of mash (if you have no corn) water and a dust bath. Continue this practice

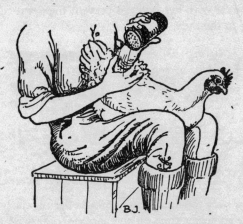

for two days until she has settled down and can be given the eggs.

If she is found standing up in the nest, then she is clearly unreliable.

It is an old custom to 'rest' sitting eggs for a day after receipt in their well-lined box by rail or post. But this is quite unnecessary.

If, however, eggs have to be kept before sitting owing to the mistiming of the broody then they should be set in bran (or remain in the box) with their large ends – containing the air cell – upwards.

If laid on their sides, they should be turned every 12 hours, to prevent the germ cell from sticking, and this can be effected by tilting or turning over the box.

When giving the hen the sitting eggs wait till she has settled down comfortably. Remove the dummy eggs from underneath her and then put the hatching eggs under her. If she is a 'pecker' put the eggs in with the back of the hand uppermost and see that she covers them all.

She will, however, re-arrange them herself with her beak after you have left her and every few hours give them a good shuffle with her body to prevent the germ cells from sticking to the shell.

'lifting her—
off the nest'　　B.J.

Sitting Boxes, Dust bath, Water, Grit & Greens.

It now only remains for you to feed her regularly and to give her sufficient time off to evacuate, otherwise the eggs will be soiled and must be washed in warm water, as also in the case of any that are broken.

A broken egg may be the sign of a clumsy broody, but it is equally the indication of the tight sitter's instinct to eliminate weak shelled eggs.

When taking the hen off it is necessary to shut the front of the coop as otherwise she may return at once.

If three sitters are released at once they are certain to squabble but no harm will be done and in two or three days they will become quite friendly. But give them plenty of feeding trough space and let them eat their fill.

It sometimes happens that the busy poultry keeper forgets to return the hen and the eggs are quite cold. He need not be unduly disturbed as, provided this does not happen in the first few days, a healthy embryo is strong enough to survive it.

There is some advantage and much instruction in testing or 'candling' the eggs after the 7th or 10th day. If the eggs are placed in front of a strong light, such as a torch, with a piece of cardboard in between (with a hole cut through of

Eggs may be tested on the 8th day; by Egg Tester ①, by Electric Torch with rubber tube over bulb ② or by candle.

UNFERTILE   ADDLED   BROKEN YOLK   GOOD

the shape of a small egg) it is possible to tell whether the egg is infertile or fertile.

The rest of the room must be in complete darkness as otherwise the central black spot and radiating blood vessels, appearing like a shadowy spider, will not easily be discerned by the novice.

It will be much more difficult on the first occasion if, fortunately, all the eggs are fertile, as the infertile egg stands out so clearly – the light shining straight through it – that it forms a ready means of comparison. Thus a new laid egg might be taken when testing.

The object of 'candling' is not only to remove the infertile eggs (which can be made into cakes) and, when more expert, the dead germs and rotten eggs, but to be able to amalgamate the sittings of two hens in the case of much infertility.

Few small poultry keepers practise it, not wishing to risk the chance of a single egg. But it is a fascinating process and much can be learnt from studying the small disc or air space at the top, the porosity of the shell and other factors.

After all, it is possible to mark with a pencil those eggs which are not thought will hatch and test your judgment afterwards.

In the same way it is well worth while candling or, if courageous, breaking open the eggs which fail to hatch. It may then be found that a perfectly formed chick is inside the shell, and much disappointment is felt that it has failed to tap a ring round the top of the shell and force its way out.

But 'dead-in-shell' is a common occurrence and it may occur any time after the 14th day by which time the chick is perfectly formed right down to its toenails. It is usually due to weak or inbred breeding stock or lack of grass range and deficiencies in the breeders' dietary.

It is utterly useless to assist a late chick out of the shell by helping to chip it, or as pigeon keepers have been known to do, putting a piece of stamp paper over the hole in the shell at which the chick seems stuck and forcing it to wriggle round and attack another side.

Individual late hatched chicks are, as a rule, quite useless although a whole brood may be late through the eggs having been held before hatching or some hitch during incubation.

HATCHING THE CHICKS

The normal day for a chick to hatch out is the 21st day, or

three weeks after setting. The chick may hatch by the 20th day, but the hatching should be complete by the 22nd day.

The best plan is not to take the hen off the nest for feeding after the eggs have begun to chip. But if the hatch is protracted this may mean a couple of days, or longer.

A hen will manage this stretch with ease but some people will alleviate this spell by feeding her on the nest.

It is almost impossible for any beginner to resist the temptation to look for the chicks before the process is complete. Empty shells can be removed then, but the less the chicks are disturbed the better.

In fact it is far better to leave the hen and chicks alone until the 23rd day when all the chicks should be dry – that

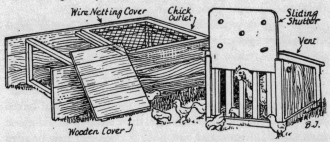

is their wet feathers will have fluffed out – and ready to be moved to the rearing coop.

If two hens are hatched off at the same time it is an obvious plan to remove all the newly hatched with one hen and leave the other to bring off the rest.

The dry chicks should be taken off in a flannel-lined basket and put in a warm place until the hen has had a good feed and a dust bath.

The same coop cannot be used for rearing as for hatching as it will not be large enough. The best size for a rearing coop is 27 in. long by 20 in. deep and 21 in. high in front.

It should have a loose floor of boards which fits flush. Chicks do not like wet or rats.

It is also a good plan to provide a small wood and wire run for the first week, so that the chicks cannot stray away from the coop.

The coop should be placed on *short* grass and after the first two days moved a yard daily.

If a lawn is not available clean earth, gravel or even fine ashes are suitable.

The chicks will not be very active for the first two days, and need little food.

Beginners are naturally anxious to tempt their chicks to eat. But they are provided with emergency rations of yolk which lasts them for three days. All they want to start with is water so that the fountain can be put inside the coop for the first day and a little fine grit or sand put down.

The coop floor should not be littered with hay or straw as the chicks get caught up in it and trampled on. Sand or even clean earth or fine ashes are preferable.

FEEDING CHICKS

In pre-war days a very good first feed consisted of baked and crumbled bread which was then steeped in skimmed milk and light squeezed out. But no foods can now be used which are fit for human consumption.

Balancer meal is fortunately an excellent alternative as with fresh grass, or a little minced green food, it forms a complete food, although to make it entirely foolproof when the birds are on poor grass the following addition should be made to 2 lb. of Balancer meal: ½ teaspoonful of salt, 4 teaspoonsful of ground chalk, 6 teaspoonsful cod liver oil, 8 teaspoonsful of dried yeast.

The mash should be fed moist and crumbly but not sloppy so as to stick to the beaks or feathers and only a very little is needed for the first week.

Four feeds daily can be given for the first month and three times afterwards.

The mash should be given for the first few days on a flat piece of wood or chick box lid and afterwards in small hoppers. No food should be left lying about to be trampled upon by the chicks.

This is easily done because for the first ten days the chick's appetite is infinitesimal.

A rubber band stretched lengthways round the trough.

After ten days the troughs can be put a little distance from the coops so that the hen cannot have more than one or two feeds a day. Dust her after a month, changing the litter every three days, but do not let her out of the coop.

It seems cruel, but except in favourable circumstances such as a well-wired orchard an uncooped hen will take the

chicks where they should not go and her scratching will cause chaos in the vegetable beds.

After a month, if she can be let out, she will find much free food for her brood and teach them to scratch and range.

The chief danger to chicks is infections picked up by continuously running over stale droppings and manured ground.

They do not need pampering, but the more often the coop litter is cleared out and the ground changed the healthier they will keep.

Chicks without the hen do little damage to the garden for the first six weeks and will greatly benefit from ranging over it.

They should be encouraged to eat green food and accustomed to an eventual house scrap diet, by including well-minced kitchen waste in the mash after the first few weeks.

Raw minced carrot is a most valuable feed, as also is fresh minced green food such as lettuce.

All remnants of porridge and milk puddings, gravy, meat stock and particularly fish and meat remnants, form excellent supplements.

The object should be to give rather concentrated and easily digested food during the first eight weeks when appetite is not so large and rapid body growth demands protein.

Thereafter more bulky food can be included such as mashed potato.

WHAT WILL A CHICK EAT?

Pre-war estimates cannot be closely followed when waste food is fed and the only reliable guide is the appetite of the chicks themselves.

But beginners must not be misled by the plaintive chirping of chicks between meals. A healthy chick is usually hungry and provided it has had all it can eat in one 'session' at meal times it can hunt for itself in between.

It is most important that it should do so and those poultry keepers with range should let their chicks out as early as possible in the morning and, if it can be arranged, not feed them for an hour or two.

On *pre-war* mash and grain the chick's consumption was: First week, 1.6 oz.; second week, 3.2 oz.; third week, 4.8 oz.; fourth week, 6.4 oz.

1st month's consumption	..	..	1 lb.
2nd ,, ,,		..	2.6 lb.
3rd ,, ,,		..	4.5 lb.
4th ,, ,,		..	5 lb.
5th ,, ,,		..	6 lb.
6th ,, ,,		..	7.5 lb.

Total consumption until lay (6th month) – 26.6 lb.; but heavy breeds (R.I.R., Sussex) may eat up to 30 lb.

Under post-war conditions, with bulky supplementary foods, these estimates will, of course, be very considerably exceeded. It is generally estimated that it takes a ton and a quarter of *rationed* food to rear 100 pullets to maturity, or 28 lb. each.

After six weeks the hen must be removed, as otherwise the chicks will not receive enough air and will not feather properly.

The chicks can be left to roost in the coop for another week if necessary on a good bedding of peat moss or straw chop. But the sooner they are provided with more air by transferring to a rearing ark or laying house the better.

Details of this stage will be found under 'GROWING PULLETS'.

BUYING DAY-OLD CHICKS

The cost of a good commercial pullet chick from a reputable firm is 1/6. The beginner can pay more but he should not pay less.

The chicks will arrive in a cardboard box neatly lined with hay. They may have travelled a long time but they will arrive quite chirpy. This is because of their 'iron ration' of yolk which they absorbed just before hatching and which enables them to do without food for three days – from the time of hatching.

The first thing to do is to get them into the warmth under

a hen or brooder. We will deal with the hen first because a hen, if obtainable, teaches both her owner and her chicks the way to go on.

A hen or pullet will take to the chicks even if she has only been sitting a day or two. But the initial introduction is always a ticklish moment because there is always the maddening broody which pecks – and pecks indiscriminately at chick or owner.

The best thing to do after dusting the hen and putting her in the coop prepared beforehand (which she will at once make great efforts to get out of) is to provide her with a chick.

This chick should be inserted quietly, back of the hand uppermost, and the coop front shut at once.

The first feed

It does not matter if the chick is not under the hen; in fact there is a danger with agitated broodies of her treading on it.

Nor is it necessary to put the chicks under at night. It is better to do so during the day so that the owner can return in half-an-hour by which time the hen should have settled down in the quiet and darkness and be brooding the chick. If she has not then, it is a case of another broody or a brooder such as is subsequently described.

If she has settled there should then be no difficulty in putting in the rest of the chicks. Again there is no necessity to thrust them under the hen. If they are placed round her she will soon have them under her, if the owner goes away at once and shuts the front again.

A further visit should be made in a short time to see that no chick is out in the cold or tucked away in some corner. A good big hen will, after April, easily brood 20 chicks if there happens to be a hitch in broody arrangements.

After the chicks have settled down a water fountain can be put just inside or outside the coop and a little meal scattered on a sheet of paper or board as mentioned previously under 'Feeding Chicks'.

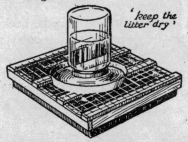

' keep the litter dry '

The water fountain should not be one which is easily tipped up or gets the chicks damp.

After a week it can be raised on a small platform so that the litter cannot be scratched into it. A little sand or fine grit should also be provided.

BROODERS

Whilst the broody hen obviously provides the most foolproof method of rearing day-old chicks, she is not always available at the time she is most wanted, in March and April. Modern laying strains have the broodiness factor largely bred out of them.

Recourse must thus be made to artificial broodies which are of many kinds, but answer to the generic title of brooders.

The beginner starting with 12 or 24 chicks need only consider three main types – the wooden box brooder, warmed by a Putnam type oil heater; the Pyramid hover, heated by oil lamp or electrical coil; and the hot water bottle brooder.

Of these, perhaps the Putnam brooder is the most suitable for very small numbers. Some novices are under the impression that chicks do not require any extra heat at all, perhaps because they arrive so bobbish in their chick box.

When Chicks are started indoors, they enjoy scratching over a fresh green sod occasionally.

The fact is that chicks can be reared quite satisfactorily in a hay box, which is a box packed with hay. But there is a danger that in cold weather the chicks may be coddled or packed too tightly and not receive sufficient air, so that the hot water bottle type is preferable.

The general principle to observe is that a chick wants plenty of heat when actually in the brooder, as well as plenty of air (and not poisonous monoxide fumes from the lamp). *But she should have every opportunity of getting out in the cold fresh air and sunlight.*

The quicker the chick is warmed up in the brooder the quicker she will go outside again – as is the case of a hen and a brood of chicks.

Thus the practise of coddling chicks inside the owner's house where they have no access to direct sunlight – a most important point – is very reprehensible.

They can be kept there for a few days, certainly but to keep them indoors for three or four weeks and perhaps put them near the kitchen stove at night and subject to floor draughts all day is the forerunner of rickets, bad feathering and probably a disease like coccidiosis when they eventually get outside.

THE PUTNAM BROODER consists of a small metal heater which burns a tiny flame and only requires refilling with oil once a week. It is placed inside an oblong wooden box which can be home-made.

This box is usually 3 ft. 9 in. long by 18 in. wide and a foot deep. There is a small slat tacked along the inside, 7 in. from the floor. The lid over the heater slides along this rail.

When the chicks are first put in – and the brooder could if necessary take up to 65 chicks to start with – they are put round the Putnam heater with a lid over their heads and a curtain on the run side.

After two days the curtain is opened and the lid slid half an inch away from the back. This allows more air under the heater and this gap is gradually widened.

The brooder box can be put on the floor of a house which

will afterwards serve the chicks for laying. After a few days the chicks can have the run of the house floor and after 10 days can run outside.

If the chicks are gradually cooled off they will feather well and the lamp can be put out by the fifth week or even earlier in the summer.

To do this, the brooder box should not be removed but the chicks encouraged to perch on top by running broad 3-inch wide perches (with bevelled edges and 1 in. deep) across the top of the brooder. When all the chicks are perching the perch can be raised and the box removed.

"Golden" movable slat floored
Colony house with hover and Wire run

To get them to perch at night it may be advisable to put the last feed of mash at night in a trough on the perches. This is the practice adopted by a leading Lancashire breeder, Mr James Sutton.

THE PYRAMID HOVER is the most popular brooder with the commercial poultry keeper. It consists, as its name implies, of a pyramid-shaped canopy usually of metal with exit holes for the fumes of the oil lamp, if it is used instead of electricity. The canopy rests on a square of wood or a circle of metal supported on legs. The sides are shut in with curtains which are removed as the chicks require more air.

The hover is again put in a house which may be the eventual laying house or it may be a small 6 ft. by 4 ft. house on wheels which is moved about the lawn with an outside run attached.

It is important that the house should have no floor draughts and it is best to place the hover on a wire netting platform – which can be purchased with the brooder – and this platform covered with a piece of sacking for the first few days.

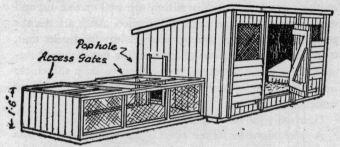

This type of brooder is rather more elaborate and expensive than is justified for 12 chicks. Yet it is foolproof, durable and easy to manage, provided there are no floor draughts.

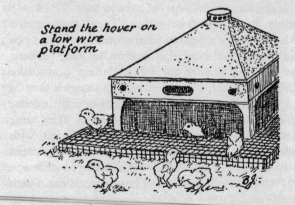

The smallest size is about 18 in. square, but it is probably better to use the 24-inch size even for a few chicks. There are also several types of small metal hovers which are specially constructed for small broods of chicks.

When the chicks are first put in they cluster round the lamp and although a thermometer is provided, and this should register 90° for the first week, the reaction of the chicks themselves provides the best guide.

If they are packed close up to the lamp they are too cold or there is a floor draught; if they are well spread out and not panting, they are correctly brooded. After a week the temperature is dropped to 85° and 5° every week after that.

A wire guard or piece of linoleum or metal should surround the hover for the first few days to keep the chicks under the brooder and the food and water be placed just under the curtains.

Gradually the floor area is extended.

A chick increases its size eight times in the first six weeks and manufacturer's specifications are always based on the number of chicks a brooder will take at a day old. Hence provided a brooder has sufficient reserve of heat the fewer the chicks placed under it the better they will do.

There are also several types of lawn or movable brooders commonly known as *foster-mothers*. These give excellent results as they have a broody compartment and one or two covered feeding and exercising sections for bad weather.

They are very readily portable and have proved their merit over many years. Their only disadvantage is that they are a specialised unit. They rear chicks to eight weeks to perfection. But they can do nothing further. They are an unnecessary expense for anyone rearing only a few chicks, and second-hand models are often faulty in the lamp section.

Lastly we come to the *hot water bottle brooder* which is again used in the poultry house or any house which can provide an outside run. Even a greenhouse would do, but a greenhouse is not the best for poultry as it is subject to temperature extremes and does not admit *direct* sunlight.

To make the hot water bottle brooder the directions of Mr L. C. Turnill, the Assistant Poultry Instructor for Kent, are invaluable.

Get a wooden box, he says, not less than 1 ft. square and 8 in. deep. It need not be square, but should not be less than 10 in. across.

If you make a box for yourself, construct it 12 in. by 1 ft. 4 in. and 9 in. deep.

At one end make a hole 4 in. square for the chicks to run in and out.

Cover this hole with a few strips of old flannelette, ½ in. wide. These should be pinned at the top with drawing-pins and loose at the bottom, so that the chicks can push in and out, as under the feathers of their mother hen.

Now buy some 'dowel' sticks or thin wooden curtain-rods. You will need to cut these into three lengths each about 2 in. longer than your box is wide.

Now make six holes in each side of the box large enough for the rods to pass through.

Three holes should be made 4 in. above the bottom of the box, the first one 4 in. from the back or end away from the pophole, the other two at 4 in. intervals. The other three should be 2 in. above the first three.

The sticks, when in place through these holes, are to carry the hot water bottle: at first in the lower holes and as the chicks grow in the upper ones.

To prepare for the chicks, put the sticks in place and wads of hay or wood-wool round the sides and blank end of the box beneath the sticks, and so as to leave a nest about 8 in. across with about 2 in. of hay at the blank end and open at the pophole end.

USE A BLANKET. About 1 in. of hay should be placed on the bottom of the nest.

Now take a piece of old blanket or flannelette a little larger than the box and pin it with drawing-pins just above

the pophole, so that it cannot slip down, and lay it over the
dowel sticks so that it covers in the nest.

The hot water bottle is placed on this above the nest.
Above the bottle, which can be rubber or stone, place more
blankets or an old cushion to keep in the heat.

· The bottle will need filling with hot water about twice a
day. If filled at about 10 o'clock at night it will last till
morning.

The bottle should not cover the whole of the nest.

There should be a few inches at the pophole end of the

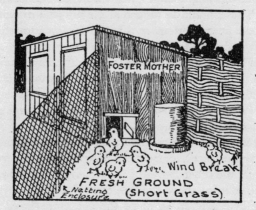

nest, which is covered only by the quilts. This allows the
chicks to choose the heat they require.

Generally, when the bottle is first filled, they will keep
away from it; as it cools, they will work underneath. At first
they are best shut in the box at night by pinning a piece of
open cloth, such as old curtain or net, over the pophole.
When two or three days old this is unnecessary.

The chicks should not be fed inside, but should have a
feeding-pen made outside.

An easy method is to have a ring of cardboard or roofing
felt round the pophole for the first week or so. After this

they can have a larger run or can go outside on short grass in fine weather.

For this you can carry the box outside and have a small wire pen round it.

It is best, however, to have a coop or other weatherproof house for the box, as it may come on to rain when you least expect it.

If your box is a stout one, a sheet of roofing felt about a yard square can be placed over the box, making a sort of tent, or even an old umbrella will do.

If you cannot get hay or wood-wool, several thicknesses of old blankets will do for the nest, and cut-up paper will do for the floor. The paper will need changing more often than the hay.

As the chicks grow, less hay is needed, so that the nest is made bigger. At about three weeks the bottle is put on to the upper holes and at four to five weeks no hot water bottle should be needed, the box being covered by the blanket or cushion only.

At this time the box may get a little wet inside during the night. If this happens, you have too thick a covering on.

Only just enough is needed at the later stages to keep the chicks from crowding in a corner of the box, which they will do if too cold.

BUYING 4 WEEK-OLD CHICKS

When chicks are purchased at 4 weeks old they still require heat – if only to prevent them from bunching at night. The two sketches reproduced herewith show how this can be done: (a) in a large house and (b) in a special Growers-on ark devised by a famous hatchery group near Hebden Bridge, Yorkshire.

WEANING CHICKS

The importance of fresh air and clean litter are the two

points which need special watching when the chicks are weaned from hen or brooder at 6 to 8 weeks.

The atmosphere in a coop occupied by a hen and chicks at 6 weeks of age in hot weather becomes very stuffy in the morning if they are not let out early. The sooner the chicks

are moved to a larger house and taught to perch the better.

Some people say that early perching leads to crooked breast bones. It may accentuate a tendency in this direction but poor bone formation is the result of bad brooding and a deficiency in feeding.

In our view the sooner the chicks get off the litter and out of the habit of bunching in a corner at night the better.

If the chicks are moved from a brooder or coop to the laying house it is a good plan to nail broad 3-inch perches to a sloping wire frame which is leant against a wall of the house with the lower end on the ground..

The wire frame consists of 1-inch mesh 17 gauge netting and prevents the chicks from getting into the corners.

By having the lowest perch on the ground they soon learn the habit of getting on to them. And since every pullet is ambitious and wants to get to the top rung of the ladder they automatically spread themselves out.

Each growing pullet should be allowed 6 in. of perch-room and as much change of ground and litter as possible.

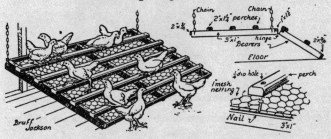

If the chicks after weaning are moved into arks – which are low apex-shaped houses with slatted floors as described under housing for layers – it is necessary to stop them from crowding into the corners at night.

As many as 75 chicks can be put in an ark of 6 ft. by 3 ft. at 6 weeks or not more than 50 at 8 weeks. But if only 12 or 20 are put in, the corners must be boarded off. The same sized ark will take 25 pullets from 12 weeks to maturity.

If the chicks are put into the ark in very cold weather a hurricane lamp could be hung from the roof for a couple of nights and straw put on the slats, which will gradually work through, or failing that, sacking.

The two rearing troubles most experienced by small

poultry keepers are feather picking and a disease delighting in the formidable title of 'coccidiosis'.

Feather picking is a cannibalistic vice often caused by over-heating and overcrowding in the brooder stage so that the feathers have no inducement to grow. It is also the result of deficiencies in the food, particularly of fish or meat, bone meal, skim milk, dried grass and minerals.

The small poultry keeper should keep his birds active and well fed by throwing in a sod of turf and such food as dandelion, chickweed, boiled nettles, lettuce, a split swede.

Few chicks that receive cooked fish trimmings suffer from any checks.

The second trouble, *coccidiosis*, is an infection of the bowels, usually distinguished by blood in the droppings, loose feathering and general inertia. It develops as a rule at about six weeks.

Chicks from poor breeding stock are more prone to it than others and it breaks out sometimes after a spell of wet weather.

The remedy as described in the Disease chapter is to move the bird *daily* on to fresh ground which really means rearing in fold pens and to change the litter also daily.

DISTINGUISHING THE SEX

Most small poultry keepers are wise in buying all pullet

chicks if they are short of house scraps. But those who can get any quantity like rearing some cockerels.

In that case they either buy the cockerels separately or buy chicks of mixed sexes ('guaranteed not sexed') at a day old. If the chicks are of both sexes the cockerels want separating as soon as they can be distinguished, because they take the food from the growing pullets. When separated they can be kept on more bulky waste food, such as potatoes, whilst the more concentrated Balancer meal can be reserved for the pullets.

The simplest method of distinguishing the sex is by the development of the comb. In 'light' breeds and crosses, that is, Leghorns, the cockerel's comb and wattles (the fleshy gills underneath the beak) develop at a month.

In heavy breeds, such as Rhode Island Reds and Sussex, the cockerel's comb development is not so noticeable until they are 8 or 10 weeks old. Even then it is not always obvious and other signs must be studied.

The tail is the best guide. In Rhode Island Reds and Sussex the cockerel's tail, contrary to expectation, does not develop as quickly as the pullets. It is very short and downy at eight weeks, like a blob, whilst the pullet's tail is better feathered, especially at the root.

Other characteristics are less obvious without experience. A cockerel does not feather so well, especially over the back. He is leggier, thicker headed, bigger and bolder. He will be the first to come to the feeding trough while the shy pullets will be more diffident.

In Rhode Island Reds some cockerels will be so indistinguishable from pullets that they will be unrecognised by the beginner until they are three or four months old. It can be assumed, however, that in a batch of mixed chicks the cockerels will outnumber the pullets and then there will be no disappointment.

As indicated in a previous chapter, if the chicks are from a sex-linked cross, i.e. Rhode Island Red cock (gold), Light Sussex hens (silver), the sex is told at once by the down colour. All the cockerels will resemble Light Sussex and all the pullets light coloured Rhode Island Reds.

But this does not apply to crosses using Leghorns, such as Black Leghorn cock × Rhode Island Red hen. Here the quick growth of the comb will provide an early pointer.

The poultry keeper should use his powers of observation, not only in recognising the sex but in noting the health and general appearance of the chicks. It will prove of inestimable value to him not only in recognising disease at once but in buying chicks.

BUYING AT 8 WEEKS OLD

We have already recommended that if chicks are not bought at day old they should be obtained at 3 months rather than 8 weeks. The reason is that they will be well feathered and fully hardened off, and it is easy to spot any weaknesses then, such as stunted growth, drooping wing, the stilted gait of rickets.

But in war time, few rearers can keep the chicks as long

as this and prefer to sell them at 8 weeks or even 4 weeks. At the later age they still need some brooding – see sketch of Thornber 'carry-on' brooder with hurricane lamp – and their feathering will look a little rough as they are changing their feathering. A chick moults, but not noticeably, half a dozen times before it is fully matured.

A Rhode Island Red × Light Sussex pullet should weigh $1\frac{1}{2}$ lb. at 2 months; $2\frac{1}{4}$ lb. at 3 months; $3\frac{1}{4}$ lb. at 4 months. Breeds with Leghorn crosses in them should weigh $\frac{1}{2}$ lb. less.

At 8 weeks the pullet should be more even in appearance, although lighter in colour than it will be at maturity.

It should have a solid little body, a bright, clean head and eye and a firm pair of legs.

Examine for signs of lice, especially about the head, as indicated by rough feathering or bare patches. It is often experienced in new hatched chicks through not dusting the broody. Dust in a pinch of sodium fluoride or 'Pulvex' (derris) avoiding the eyes.

BUYING 3 MONTHS OLD

At 3 months old a pullet should feel waxy in feather, solid in body with its wings well clipped into its sides – not drooping or hanging out. The breast bone should be quite straight with no kinks or curves which indicates rickets (and not early perching). The back should be flat, not roached, and the tail straight, not 'wrytailed' in which case it is held to one side.

When examining the head, open the beak to make sure that it is clean with no yellow canker or patches on tongue or down the gullet or unpleasant smell.

There should also be no moisture in the nostrils, or in the eye, as these are all signs of colds.

There should be no scabs, or whitish lumps on the head and the rump feathering should be quite clean.

Loose yellow droppings are a sign of indigestion which may be temporary but it may also be the sign of an infection, so the benefit of the doubt should not be given. The shanks should not be too thin and the toes quite straight.

But no word picture can really convey the indefinable differences between a pullet of stamina and quality and one of doubtful vigour.

It is a case when the Domestic Poultry-keepers' Council with its Club experts and its local organisers can be of incalculable personal assistance to the novice.

It should also be added that the Poultry Press provides a free approval system which protects the buyer against an unsatisfactory purchase.

'POINT OF LAY' PULLETS

It is almost impossible in war time to buy pullets at 5 or 6 months except at very high prices. In any case the expression 'point of lay' as used by dealers of doubtful integrity very seldom means what it implies.

A pullet comes into lay at any time from $4\frac{1}{2}$ months to 8 months. Its comb 'springs' and turns from a pale pink to a bright red about ten days or a fortnight before this exciting event. The pelvic bones, the ends of which can be felt on either side of the vent, widen and the abdomen fills out. The pullet shows increasing interest in her food, is constantly ranging, and begins prating.

If the pullet starts laying as early as $4\frac{1}{2}$ months, it is either very early hatched, as in January, or it has been constantly fed instead of being allowed to search for a proportion of natural food; or, *it is a strain or cross which has not been bred for slow maturity.*

But there is no disadvantage in this early maturity providing food is given generously and, if possible, contains fish waste. Otherwise they will 'neck' moult and go out of lay.

WHEN THE PULLETS ARRIVE

There is one elementary step to take when pullets arrive and that is to examine them closely, then put them straight into the house and keep them there for a day and a night. They will then know their home.

If you drop them in the run, if you have one, there is always the possibility that they may fly up to a tree to roost or even escape.

Poultry are creatures of habit. Once they acquire a habit it is very difficult to break them of it, whether it is egg eating or laying on the floor or roosting in the nest box.

FIRST EGGS

Nests should always be put in the darkest corner and well littered. If pullets are found laying on the ground, if possible, catch them and put them gently in the nest.

Pullets when they first start to lay often provide 'wind' eggs, i.e. a little white just covered with shell or soft-shelled eggs. They are most easily noticed on the dropping board. Unless these are persistent there is nothing to worry about.

But a chronic layer of a soft-shelled or double-yolked egg has probably some inherent defect which may be impossible to put right.

The egg organs are a very complicated piece of mechanism. The ripe yolk ruptures a thin membrane and slips into the mouth of the oviduct. If, through some defect, or sudden shock such as gunfire, the yolk fails to drop into the oviduct but falls in the body of the abdomen it is followed by others and the bird dies of peritonitis.

In the passage of the yolk down the oviduct it is covered with 'white' and shell.

A sudden shock, or an inability to assimilate calcium (cockle shell, green food) may prevent the white from receiving its full complement of layers of shell, hence the soft-shelled egg.

Some particle of foreign matter passing down the oviduct may be mistaken for a yolk and be covered with white and shell.

A yolk may be in the oviduct when the pullet is suddenly frightened and the yolk instead of going down goes back, giving another yolk and forming a double-yolked egg. Alternatively it may be retained and be laid hard boiled.

But considering the incidents which might happen to an egg, they very seldom do, and the stronger the pullet the less the chance of a mishap.

Also the glossier and closer knit the texture of the egg shell, the healthier the pullet.

MOULTING

If a pullet comes into lay when not fully matured in body, nature often calls a halt after a few eggs and the pullet either moults or goes broody.

It may not be the full moult which a spring-hatched pullet undergoes in August and September after its year of lay. It may moult its neck feathers only.

The more protein, such as fish waste, that it can be given the quicker its body will develop and it will return to lay.

BROODINESS

Broodiness in young pullets again can be attributed to lack of bodily development. Since broodiness gives hens a rest from laying it is not altogether to be discouraged in either growing pullets or breeding hens. But it takes time and food and nest box space, and must be dealt with.

The chief essential in obtaining a rapid cure is to remove the bird from the nest directly she is detected. If a bird stays on the nest at roosting time; if she ruffles up her feathers and squawks, she should not be given the benefit of the doubt.

She should be removed to a slatted coop where she is provided with a generous allowance of mash and given a good dusting. Or she can be put in another run, if one is available, and even given a young cockerel as a companion.

A perch will do as a house and in five days, in her anxiety to get back to her old nest, she will cure herself.

WHEN TO KILL COCKERELS

If cockerels are reared for table at the same time as the pullets they are obviously killed off as rations dictate.

But it is as well to know the economic time to kill them. This, under a full mash ration, which a wartime cockerel did not get, is 16 weeks. If the bird is very largely reared on potatoes and grass then there will not be much on its gaunt frame at 4 months. It could be left to 5 months. But after this it eats more food than its slow weight increase justifies.

It also crows vigorously, which is to be deprecated if back-yarders want to keep on good terms with their neighbours.

WHEN TO CULL HENS

It is equally necessary – and one of the most important points in poultry keeping – to know when to kill either pullets or hens. If a bird 'dies on you' or is picked up feeling very light or grossly heavy or fat the owner must blame himself for his lack of observation.

WEED OUT ~

THE OLD AND FAT →

THE TOO EARLY MOULTER ↙

THE ASTHMATIC ↗

THE UNDER-SIZED "SMALL-EGGER" ↙

THE "BROODY ONCE TOO OFTEN" ↘

AND ANY HEN "DOWN BEHIND" ←

Braffackson

It is hard for the beginner to be ruthless. It is the most difficult and valuable lesson he can learn. There are only a very few troubles, such as mild colds or scaly legs, or even a light attack of coccidiosis, which pay to cure.

One of the best guides to health is appetite. A hungry hen is a laying hen. Feeding time affords the best chance of picking out 'duds' or, as they are technically called, 'culls'.

A bird that hangs about in the background, diffidently picking, is a bird that can be 'outed' without hesitation. It may have worms, a tumour, or some other infection which if left will be quickly passed on.

It is a novice's instinct to fly to the medicine chest. But castor oil and most internal disinfectants are valueless and even dangerous in the poultry run. Prevention in the shape of sound stock, good food and clean runs is the best cure.

It is worth while, however, having a post-mortem examination of any bird that looks seedy, as it is a wise precaution as well as a useful lesson. But such a post-mortem must be conducted by a skilled poultry pathologist as there may be more than one ailment and only the microscope and the blood smear and culture will reveal the primary causes. Few veterinary surgeons have ever bothered to study the subject.

A summarised review of poultry diseases and disinfection appears in a following chapter, prepared with the co-operation of Dr H. P. Bayon, of Cambridge University.

CULLING HEALTHY YEARLINGS

The poultry keeper may be confronted with an equally difficult problem and that is to reduce his healthy yearlings to make room for next season's pullets.

Firm, Satiny Comb & Wattles, Bright Eye, Lean, Smooth Face. Ragged Plumage

Jaunty Alert Carriage

Moist, White Vent. Colourless Lean Legs.

Young birds should not be mixed with old birds until they are mature enough to stand up for themselves at the mash trough.

This dual penning places a great strain on accommodation.

Statistics show that in large units it only pays to retain 25 per cent of the yearlings for another year, as if the yearly flock average for the pullets is 180 it may not exceed 140 for the hens.

Which yearlings to kill? The small poultry keeper who

uses his eyesight has a great advantage here over the large farmer.

He knows which hens lay best by recognising their eggs. But here are a few signs of a heavy layer.

First out in the morning, last to go to roost, always hungry, active, ranging, rough in feather, bleached in leg and eye pigment, late moulting, no thickness about the abdomen when picked up and gently squeezed.

Here are the indications in tabular form:

CULLING GUIDE

	Good Layer	Poor Layer
Vent	Bluish-white, large moist	Flesh-coloured, contracted, dry
Eyelids ..	Thin, white edges	Thick flesh-coloured
Eye	Prominent, bright	Sunken, listless
Comb and Wattles	Red, smooth, soft and glossy	Pale or yellowish, wrinkled, rough, dry
Face	Red, thin, smooth	Full, fleshy, yellowish
Beak	White	Coloured
Pelvic Bones ..	Flexible, no fat	Rigid, thick, fleshy
Shanks ..	White, thin, rough, flat	Coloured, round, smooth
Plumage ..	Tight, soiled, worn, very little fluff	Loose, new feathers or moulting, thick fluff
Skin	Velvety, loose, blue-veined, thin	Coarse, tight, dry, or greasy and underlaid with fat

In yellow-legged breeds, the word 'flesh-coloured' means yellow.

PIGMENT GUIDE

Pigmentation is to some extent a guide to the length of time a hen has been laying. The colour fades from various parts of the body, as eggs are produced.

Here is the approximate rate of fading of pigmentation:

	Noticeable fading at	Complete bleaching at
Vent	2 weeks	4 weeks
Eye ring and facial points	2 weeks	4 weeks
Beak	4 weeks	10 weeks
Shanks	8 weeks	20 weeks

HOW TO BOIL AN EGG

Having at last succeeded in winning the fruits of the poultry endeavour it is surprising how few people know how to boil an egg.

It is essential that the water should completely cover the eggs, otherwise they cook unevenly. Slip them in gently off the spoon to avoid cracking.

THREE METHODS

1. Put into boiling water and boil for three minutes; if very fresh, or if individual taste requires the white to be fairly firm, allow $\frac{1}{2}$ to 1 minute more.
2. Place in boiling water; when the water boils again, put on the lid, remove the saucepan to a warm spot so that the water keeps hot, but not boiling, and leave for ten minutes.
3. Place in cold water, bring slowly to boiling-point, and remove immediately the water boils.

By the two latter methods, eggs are 'lightly' boiled and are therefore more digestible.

Cracked eggs may be boiled satisfactorily by rubbing the

shell over with lemon juice, or sticking a piece of gummed paper over the crack.

HOW TO KILL

Although left to the last, the unpleasant task of killing hens and chicks must be grasped. How many poultry runs and poultry flock have suffered heavy losses simply because the owner, through a natural squeamishness or lack of knowledge, has put this job off?

Let us take the chick first. Its poor little neck is too fragile to stretch and dislocate as with any bird over two months.

So put its neck up against a sharp edge of a door or table and press the thumb nail on the other side. This will sever the neck bone and death will be instantaneous, although the nerves will cause spasms and fluttering.

With the adult, take its legs – and its wings if you like – in one hand and its head in the other. Grip just behind the head with the first finger and thumb, or if your fingers are strong the first and second fingers.

Thrust the head back and give a good firm pull until you feel a sudden 'give'. This will indicate the parting of the neck bone just below the head and the blood will drain if you hang the bird head downwards. There will be strong fluttering and spasmodic reflexing of the legs but do not be deterred. This shows that you have made a job of it. If you pull the head off – well, it's better than half pulling it and allowing the cockerel to run off.

HOW TO DETECT AND TREAT POULTRY DISEASES

ANAEMIA. Pale combs and wattles. Many different causes; unhealthy surroundings, badly ventilated housing, unsuitable feeding; red mites at night, worms. Remedy consists in finding cause of ill-health and removing it.

BACILIARY WHITE DIARRHOEA. *Chicks:* White liquid droppings voided with painful squeaks; die between three and seven days; vents closed by dry white droppings. In chronic cases (adult) ovary usually ill-developed. Bacteriological examination should decide.

Disinfect all metal appliances with blow lamp; scrub all wooden appliances with a solution of 1 in 10 washing soda, followed by a coating of reliable antiseptic. Cull all weaklings. Put remainder on fresh litter and get them into the open as soon as feasible; afterwards dig up and rest grass runs for three months. Blood-test survivors at 3 months of age.

BLACK GUT results in sudden death of several pullets or hens. The bowels are loaded with a black pigment due to irritation induced by harmful additions to the drinking water, such as vinegar and metal sulphates, etc. The condition will develop several weeks after tampering with the water.

BLINDNESS OR PINHEAD PUPIL. May be due to different causes; cull out birds and obtain expert advice. Condition does not spread by contact.

BLOOD-SPOTS in eggs. These are usually laid by some particular hen or hens – which should be isolated and watched, for the blood-spots may be a danger signal of later trouble. If not, it will cease on its own by reduced feeding.

BREAST BLISTERS. Caused by fowls fidgeting on floor' or wire netting. Rub with vaseline; provide suitable perches.

BUMBLEFOOT. Usually deposit of uric acid salts or gout, Revise diet; give exercise. If due to tuberculosis, do not treat, destroy birds.

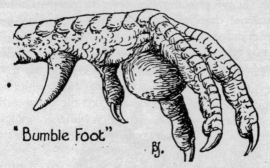

"Bumble Foot"

CANNIBALISM; FEATHER-PICKING; TOE-PECKING. Overcrowding, overheating and/or food deficiency in quality, not quantity. Provide space, ventilation and, especially, meat or fish waste and green food in mash. Apply

Feather Eating.

iodine or Stockholm tar to affected parts. Remove pecked birds.

COCCIDIOSIS. Coccidia microscopical: multiply in walls

of bowels, several varieties. All dangerous, spread easily.

Chicks: Drooping wings; drowsy; blood-stained droppings; mortality usually from a fortnight. *Adults:* Leg weakness; pale comb, unthrift.

Move chicks to fresh ground *daily*; employ fold pens. In brooder house provide wire floor to prevent access to droppings or change litter daily. Give good mash, preferably containing skim milk, and cod-liver oil.

COLDS (Bacterial Roup). Heavy breathing; swollen or gummed-up eyes; clogged nostrils. *Treatment:* Give 2 per

cent cod-liver oil in mash (3 teaspoonfuls to 1 lb.) Do not overcrowd. Plenty of fresh air; watch ventilation at night. Many dangerous disease outbreaks, may start with what appear to be 'colds' so do not neglect condition.

CROOKED BREASTBONE. Lack of Vitamin D, or coccidiosis. Add cod-liver oil to growers' mash.

CROP-BINDING. Due to indigestion from many causes, such as coccidia, worms, misuse of salts or disinfectants, long fibrous grass; also gizzard or bowel stoppage by tuberculosis, ovarian tumours, excess of fat, retained yolks, etc.; see Sour Crop. Give a dose of water and olive oil in equal parts of milk.

If this fails, kill, since a surgical operation, whilst simple, seldom achieves permanent results.

DEPLUMING MITES. See under Lice and Mites.

DISINFECTANTS IN DRINKING WATER. Avoid com-

Abnormal 'Croppy' Hen

pletely. Disinfect buildings and appliances, but do not add poison to feeds. See Black Gut.

DOUBLE YOLKS mean that hen is producing yolks too fast. Reduce feeding and check laying. It may be chronic.

DROPPED VENT; PROTRUSION OF CLOACA (Prolapsus). May be due to retained soft-shelled egg, inherent weakness of muscles, etc. Isolate bird. Grease protruding gut and gently replace by pressure with pad of cotton wool. Repeat if necessary. Provide soft unstimulating mash. If ineffective, as frequently the case, kill.

DROPSY, or WATER BELLY. Abdomen swollen, featherless, red; soft feels like 'water bladder'.

DUST BATH of fine ashes mixed with 1 in 20 of flowers of sulphur. Keep dry, under good cover; prevents lice from spreading.

EGG BINDING. Swollen abdomen; if egg ruptured, penguin attitude.

Grease vent, manipulate egg gently with tips of fingers. If no result, kill.

Egg Eating

EGG EATING. Aggravated by lack of drinking water, low protein food, lack of oyster-shell, and particularly inactivity. Revise feed; place culprits, if identified, in laying battery, or more drastically nip the tip off the beaks so that they do not quite meet.

EPSOM SALTS. Single doses may be beneficial, but regular use is harmful and ruins birds' digestion.

FAT EXCESS. *Laboured breathing; blue comb, hard, swollen abdomen*. Provide exercise; reduce food, especially cereal mashes, add green food.

FEATHERING. Bare patches, such as red rumps in heavy layers, are often a sign of lack of protein such as fish or meat waste.

FEATHER MITES or **DEPLUMING MITES.** See under Lice and Mites.

FEATHER-PICKING. See Cannibalism.

FOWL PARALYSIS. Paralysis of legs, one wing, claws or neck; blind eyes or odd-shaped pupil. Recurrence can be prevented by suitable feeding of young birds (including green stuff and reliable cod-liver oil); careful selection of breeders; do not use the stock, especially **COCKERELS**, for breeding.

FOWL POX (Diphtheritic Roup or Canker). Frothy eyes. Warts on combs, corner of mouth, wing; yellow matter in mouth.

Paint outside warts with tincture of iodine. Clean away cheesy masses inside mouth with cotton-wool pellets on stick dipped in weak antiseptic. Inoculate with fowl pox vaccine obtainable from laboratories.

GAPES. See under Worms.

GIZZARD STOPPAGE THROUGH MATTED GRASS. Every summer numerous pullets waste away and die because their gizzard is blocked by hard balls of undigested grass fibre. Remedy: Keep grass short. Provide grit.

LAMENESS OR LEG WEAKNESS. May be due to lack of Vitamin D; chronic coccidiosis; worms; layers' cramp; tuberculosis, acute indigestion; light attack of fowl-paralysis.

LARYNGO-TRACHEITIS. Hissing rattle in throat; gasping for breath; sudden death. Comb dark red; congested; dribbling from mouth. Isolate early. Inform Area Organiser, or send for post mortem.

Do not overcrowd; provide for ventilation at all times; see that feed is well balanced; add cod-liver oil. Kill and burn ailing fowls.

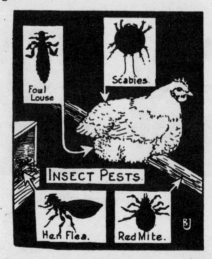

LICE, FLEAS AND BUGS. Dust birds with sodium fluoride (avoiding eyes) or 'Pulvex' (Derris). Clear out old nest-box litter and floor dust. Creosote woodwork. Provide dust bath with flowers of sulphur.

LICE AND MITES. Red mite and fleas multiply *away* from the bird, and the perches and cracks in woodwork must be treated with mixture of creosote and paraffin; lice ('creepers') breed among the feathers.

Painting perches with nicotine sulphate (perch-paint) or paraffin is effective against all lice and mites. In bad cases of feather mite dip birds in bath made of sodium fluoride 1½ oz., flowers of sulphur 4 oz., soap ½ oz., in two gallons of water.

MOULTING. Through a natural process, varying in frequency and intensity from breed to breed, a too heavy and prolonged moult is usually the result of some fault in management or quality of feeding. Obtain advice from Club Secretary or Front Line Organiser.

NEWCASTLE DISEASE or fowl pest is notifiable to the Ministry of Agriculture, New Haw, Weybridge. Recognisable by dribbling from beak and sudden death. Often starts with apparent colds.

SCALEY LEG. Caused by microscopical mite. Scrub with old toothbrush dipped in paraffin three times at 5-day intervals.

POISONING

Blood-streaked droppings; paralysis of muscles; oozing of saliva from beak; thirst; sudden death. Try to find cause or nature of poison; whether fertilizer, rat poison, vegetable poison (yew, laburnum seeds, etc.). Give diluted milk, soft mashes.

ARSENIC. From fruit sprays; weed-killer. Give flowers of sulphur in water or diluted milk, or a spoonful of ferric hydrate, at intervals, made by diluting 1 oz. of solution of ferric chloride in a wine-glass of water and adding a teaspoonful of washing soda (sodium carbonate).

PHOSPHORUS. From rat poison. Try to empty crop and pour in ten drops of turpentine in a little egg-white whipped up in 2 oz. of water. Do not give oil or milk. Magnesium sulphate as a purgative.

LEAD POISONING. From swallowing shot or bits of lead; at times present in soil and water. Teaspoonful of magnesium sulphate in half a tumbler of water. Give several spoonfuls.

RED MITES. See Lice and Mites.

SOFT-SHELLED EGGS. Provide good oyster-shell; add certified cod-liver oil (3 teaspoonfuls to 1 lb. of mash), feed greens. Cut down rations to check laying.

SOUR CROP. Excess of mash, possibly lack of grit; and many other causes which interfere with digestion. Find out and avoid cause.

TUBERCULOSIS. Going light; thin; leg weakness and lameness in one leg; droppings greenish yellow. Pale comb. No treatment. Kill, burn carcass and all droppings. Apply Tuberculin Test (obtainable from Ministry of Agriculture) to remainder and keep away from pigs and cattle. Treat soil thoroughly. Deal with scourge, do not delay as birds may go on dying at intervals for years.

TUMOURS, ESPECIALLY OF OVARY. Going light; delayed egg-laying. Do not breed from strain showing them.

TYPHOID. Evil-smelling, greenish-yellow droppings; hot legs; mortality varies, but deaths usually sudden. Bacteriological examination should decide. Complete disinfection is essential. Burn carcasses. Delay is dangerous. Blood-test layers. Occurs also in chicks. Inoculation with Vaccine will protect fowls during six months.

VENT GLEET. Yellowish, evil-smelling discharge from vent; fluff thick, sticking together. Isolate ailing birds immediately. Syringe vent with mild antiseptic, such as 5 per cent boric solution in warm water, greasing with vaseline or zinc ointment. If not effective in week – kill.

WHITE COMB (OR FLAVUS). White patches or blisters on comb. (Do not confuse with fowl pox.) Paint with tincture of iodine or employ special ointment. Give birds green food.

WORMS

Loose wings, weakness; blood-stained droppings; diarrhoea or constipation; soiled vent; straining. Wry neck in chicks, head twisted back on neck in adults; pale combs. The one sure way to recognise the cause of these ailments is to find the worms in their droppings or their eggs. Remember that every effective worm treatment is not without danger and is dependent upon success for reconditioning the ground, otherwise the worms will be picked up again.

CAECUM PIN-WORMS (Heterakis). Can be detected with a little attention; about 1 in. long and as thick as a cotton thread.

A rectal injection of 12 drops of a mixture of 1 drachm of oil of chenopodium in 6 oz. of olive oil is effective, but requires skill. For prevention recondition soil by liming, digging and resting.

Prevention is far better than any capsule.

GAPE-WORMS. Chicks cough, gasp and wheeze or continually stretch necks and open beaks; death frequent. Remove to fresh ground. Pass feather dipped in equal parts of turpentine and olive oil up and down windpipe, not gullet. Try garlic oil capsules, but above all recondition soil.

HAIR-WORMS. Can only be detected by the microscope or strong lens; about as thick as a human hair.

Dose once only with Epsom Salts, 1 lb. to 100 birds; twelve hours later give each bird 5 drops of aniseed oil in 1 teaspoonful of olive oil. After medicine has acted remove to fresh run and clean house.

ROUNDWORMS (Ascaridia). Can be seen with the naked eye; about 2 to 3 in. in length. For treatment, Carbon tetrachloride capsules effective. Recondition run and isolate affected birds.

SMALL TAPEWORMS. Pieces in droppings are small and white, can be detected by placing droppings diluted in water in a glass vessel against a dark background. Size of cotton thread, cut square. Transmitted by slugs.

Dose, once only, with Epsom Salts (tablespoonful dissolved in water and mixed in mash for six fowls); followed by thymol capsules at five-day intervals until free. Clear runs of slugs (host of tapeworm), by applying lime or agricultural sale or broadcast a mixture of one part of bluestone to 6 of sand, 5 cwts. to the acre.

DISINFECTION IN DISEASE OUTBREAKS

When disease occurs the spread of infection can be avoided by attention to these simple rules:

Prompt isolation of the diseased birds and recognition of the ailment by sending birds for post mortem to a laboratory specialising in poultry pathology.

As soon as the disease is known steps should be taken to remedy it. In the meantime, clean and disinfect the ground, appliances and houses.

Carefully watch the birds that have been in contact with the ailing ones and separate them – the moment they appear ill.

Do not add disinfectants or corroding mineral acids to the drinking water; these only lower the natural resistance of the birds to disease.

A simple but unreliable method of disinfection is the natural system; which consists in exposing an appliance, after scraping off all encrusted droppings and dirt, to the effects of the weather – open air, rain and sunshine.

But the danger always lurks in cracks, corners and crevices where sun and light cannot penetrate. Red-mite, for example, can live without food for months and certain bacteria will survive under shelter for years. As preventatives the following can be recommended:

SCRUBBING BRUSH AND HOT WASHING SODA SOLUTION. A good stiff brush with a long handle and a pail of boiling water to which is added 1 lb. of washing soda to every gallon of water, is the most effective of all disinfecting outfits.

The water should be kept boiling in a pail on a Primus Stove or Putnam heater, and the brush rinsed in it at intervals; hot washing soda solution dissolves dirt and kills germs.

Where there is caked, dry droppings and dirt, a scraper or old knife should be first used to remove all lumps; which are collected on paper and burnt. A smaller scrubbing brush can be employed for hovers, brooders or appliances; these must be separately treated, not the same dirty solution employed. When dry follow up with a good disinfectant.

SPRAY PUMP FOR DISINFECTING SOLUTIONS. Though an ordinary paint-brush is suitable for spreading disinfectants on movable appliances, like perches, etc., for the walls of buildings and above all for corners and crevices which harbour red-mites, the use of a spray-pump has advantages, since the spray will soak into cracks and joints which cannot be reached with a brush, although it is wasteful.

DISINFECTION OF HOVERS. All litter should be swept up and burnt and the wood floor first scraped and then scrubbed with a stiff brush plunged in a hot solution of washing soda (1 lb. to a gallon of water) so that every visible trace of droppings or dirt has been removed.

HOW TO CLEAN AND RECONDITION STALE GROUND. To treat fowls for worms without reconditioning the soil is waste of time, money and effort. To recondition the soil and place worm-ridden or diseased birds on it, is useless, for in a short time the parasites will again become numerous. Both methods of treatment complete each other; to be of use both are required.

To treat the runs proceed as follows: On each acre spread a dressing of 1 ton of lime (i.e. hydrate lime, burnt lime, slaked lime, or 2 tons of limestone dust or flour) or 6 cwt. of agricultural salt, or 6 cwt. of Kainit – according to whether the soil is deficient in lime, chlorides or potash respectively. For smaller areas estimate that 1 cwt. of salt will cover 800 sq. yds.

To avoid tapeworm, and therefore the host, the common slug – add either to the salt or to the Kainit 1 cwt. of copper sulphate.

It is essential to mix sulphate with some other ingredient before applying it, as otherwise it does not spread evenly. Therefore, scatter a mixture of 1 part of bluestone to 6 of sand; about 5 cwt. an acre.

Aim, however, at covering the ground lightly but thoroughly and then digging the dressing in; the latter is by far the most important feature.

The top dressing should be allowe to lie for a week or more, till rain and weather have enabled it to unfold its activity. After this interval dig the soil up lightly – 3 in. to 5 in. deep will suffice – and then even out with a rake. Suitable grass may be seeded, and the soil raked over again; the growing roots will break up the soil. If fertilizers have been added, see that they sink into the soil, so that the fowls do not accidentally pick up some and ruin their digestions.

If infection has been present, three months at least should be allowed before hens are again placed on the ground after such treatment. To allow the ground to lie fallow, without reconditioning, is useless.

GRASS SEED MIXTURES. As a grass seed mixture for chick-runs sow: 30 lb. of wild or indigenous perennial rye grass (at 1s. 6d. a lb.), 9 lb. smooth stalked meadow grass; 9 lb. of fine-leaved agrostis; 4 lb. chewing fescue – sown at 52 lb. per acre. This mixture incidentally is also suitable for tennis-lawns.

Do not allow weedy, stringy grass to grow long in poultry runs or range. It is dangerous. – See Gizzard Stoppage. The shorter the grass is kept the more the sun, wind and rain can get at the droppings and harmful bacteria.

DUCKS

The difference between a common duck of the market-place and village pond and the pedigree Khaki Campbell and

Aylesbury is the difference between the scrub goat and the Saanen.

The common crossbred duck lays in the spring. The Khaki Campbell lays almost every day all the year round. This is no exaggeration.

In official laying tests many individual ducks have laid over 300 eggs (in forty-eight weeks) and averages of all ducks consistently exceed 250 eggs.

The best laying breed of duck is the Khaki Campbell with its off-shoot the White Campbell, although there are a few good strains of Indian Runner ducks and also of Buff Orpingtons.

But unfortunately these are now in too few hands, and the Khaki Campbell will suffice for the beginner.

The only table breed worth considering is the Aylesbury. Well-bred Aylesbury duckling will weigh up to 6 lb. at 11 weeks. Their annual average egg production is about 100 eggs and they are not good winter layers.

If ducks like Khaki Campbells are such good layers of

over $2\frac{1}{2}$ oz. and have a far lower mortality than hens, why is it that they are not more kept?

The first reason is that the laying duck is equipped with a non-stop pair of webbed feet which soon puddle restricted space.

The second is that the duck egg, whilst magnificent eating when new laid, has a rather more porous shell than a hen's egg and is liable to deteriorate more rapidly, thus causing an unjustified prejudice against strong flavour.

Now if a duck produces eight times her own weight in eggs yearly she has a pretty healthy appetite. And she likes to satisfy it, if she is given the opportunity, with as large an amount of natural food in the way of worms, slugs and frogs as she can.

Hence her activity, and her constant traversing of the ground like a speed boat rounding buoys in the Solent, in her assiduous hunt after tasty morsels.

In a small pen she soon pads the ground down to a hard cake in summer, on which only plantains will survive, and to a muddy slush in winter.

It is therefore essential to concrete a part or whole of the pen if it is very small. Or if an orchard is used, which is an ideal spot, it can be divided into two and then only special attention need be given to the entrances and ground round the drinking troughs.

Ducks do not require water to swim in, even for breeding purposes, but they do need a good sunk bath, or pool with a drainage plug in which they can wash themselves.

Nor do ducks need a house, if no foxes are about, as they will sleep out all the year round. And the wire netting need not exceed 3 ft. high.

They are highly strung, intelligent creatures which will readily respond to friendly management – coming to the owner's feeding whistle like an obedient house dog – but quickly put off by strange attendants or unusual happenings.

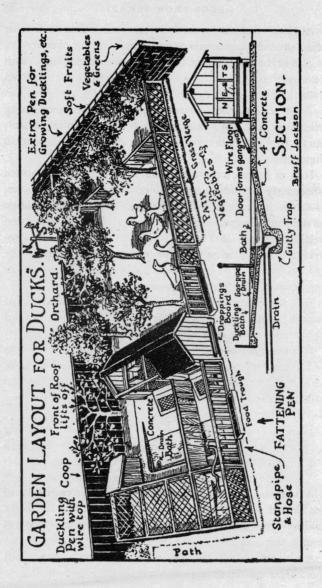

GARDEN LAYOUT FOR DUCKS.

Duckling Coop

Front of Roof lifts off

Orchard.

Duckling Pen with wire top

Extra Pen for Growing Ducklings, etc.

Soft Fruits

Vegetables & Greens

Grass Verge

PATH

Vegetables

Wire Floor

Door forms gangway

Bath

Droppings Board

Gas-pipe Drain

Ducklings Bath

4 Concrete

Gully Trap

Drain

SECTION.

Bruff Jackson

Concrete Bath

Drain

Food Trough

Standpipe & Hose

FATTENING PEN

Path

Although housing is not necessary in unfoxed areas, it offers protection in winter and is a useful means of collecting eggs. But the eggs will not be clean, house or no house, clean litter or wet.

A duck will lay its egg invariably before 8 a.m. so it can be kept in until then, thereby sacrificing the early worm. Whilst whiling away the tedium of waiting to be let out, ducks appear to play football with their eggs, so dirty do they come.

It is, of course, only the natural instinct of the wild duck whose eggs are hidden and stained for protective purposes, and it is common to find all the eggs from one pen hidden in the litter in one nest.

If the house is used it should be airy, and of simple construction, provided it offers protection from vermin.

Useful wire-floored duck house

A wire front – with a wide door – ensures plenty of ventilation and although some protection for the litter against driving rain is an advantage, the litter soon gets wet in any case.

A well-rammed earth floor is probably best, upon which some litter can be spread and frequently changed.

FEEDING

A duck can be fed on the same crumbly mash as a hen, but when in heavy lay on restricted range, needs all the food you can give it.

This, with a mash largely supplemented with kitchen waste, may be as much as 10 to 12 oz. a day.

In the absence of large quantities of worms, slugs and frogs, which it can find on range, it responds very readily to fish waste or any meat scraps or animal protein.

The duck will consume comfortably 10 oz. a day, given in two meals, of Balancer meal and scraps. But if it is on range and can get plenty of natural food its first meal will be a light one as it will be in too much of a hurry to get at the worms.

If drinkers only are provided they should be sufficiently deep to immerse the heads but not wide enough to paddle in.

HATCHING

One drake can be mated to six ducks, but the ducks make unreliable mothers.

A hen will sit on 10 duck eggs on well-moistened turf after a good dusting with insect powder and the hatch may start on the 26th day and will be complete by the 28th day.

The ducklings need not, however, be removed from the

BREED
TO
KEEP

Black Leghorn
. I. Red.

Rhode Island
.

3. Rhode Island Red cockerel—but do not keep it unless you have ample grass range for breeding.

4. Light Sussex

5. White Leghorn

6. House and scratching shed. Trellis forms neat substitute for wire netting.

HOUSING

7. 8 ft. by $4\frac{1}{2}$ ft. house suitable for six pullets kept intensively. Designed by National Utility Poultry Society, 4, Arne Street, London, W.C.2, who can supply free plan

8. Hannaford Garden Fold pen for small flock.

9. Cheap fold pen of Ruberoid roofing felt on wooden framing

10. Lawn fold pen designed by Leonard Turnill. Plan from National Utility Poultry Society, 4, Arne St., London, W.C.2

11. Indoor Battery House for twelve pullets, designed by Mr. W. L. Grice, of Spillers.

LAYING BATTERIES

12. Mr. Austin Burgess, Surrey Sub-Area Organiser, feeding fresh green stuff to his heavy laying pullets in improvised outdoor Battery

13. Rhode Island Red pullet at (R. to L.) three weeks, six weeks, nine weeks and three months.

14. Hen-rearing coops on the lawn.

REARING

15. Sex-linked chicks from Rhode Island Red cock by Light Sussex hen. (Left) Pullet chick. (Right) Cockerel chick

16. Pyramid Hover with raised floor.

BROODING

17. (Below) Putnam oil heater with Brooder box.

18. Hot water bottle brooder.

19. Thornber 'carry-on' brooder for chicks after four weeks.

20. Coccidiosis or Rickets.

21. Mis-shapen or blurred eye pupil means a bad layer.

DISEASE

22. Fowl pox.

23. Paralysis, tumours or worms.

24. Best Layer – Khaki Campbell   25. Best Table Duck – Aylesbury

DUCKS AND GEESE

26. Chinese Geese   27. Toulouse Goose

28. 2,000 bird laying battery plant and pedigree Friesians on Mr. Savage's Farm at Albury, Guildford.

FARMS OF THE FUTURE

29. Laying Folds on the Wiltshire Downs on Sykes Bros.' Farm at Tytherington.

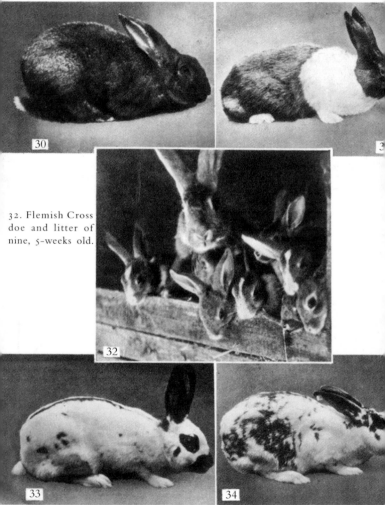

30. Flemish Giant

31. Dutch

32. Flemish Cross doe and litter of nine, 5-weeks old.

33. Old English

34. Checkered Giant

35. Chinchilla

36. Chinchilla Gigantea

37. Blue Beveren

38. Havana

39. Siamese Sable

REX FUR VARIETIES

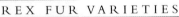

40. Chinchillarex

41. Erminerex

42. Breeding Hutches. Showing advantages of double door system

43. Growing Hutches
In stacks of eight

44. Correct Handling
Weight of rabbit on left hand

45. Sexing
Showing Male Organ

46. Outside Running-on Hutches.
Overhanging roof. Protection for stock and operator.

47. Mash.

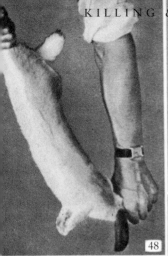

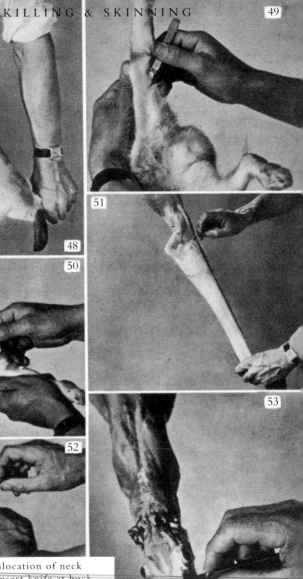

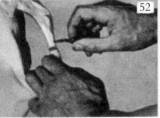

48. Killing. Dislocation of neck
49. Skinning. Insert knife at hock
50. Cutting from vent to hock of other leg.
51. Cutting any tissues impeding progress
52. Cutting skin off at hock
53. Skinning head. Keep stretched, cutting close to head.

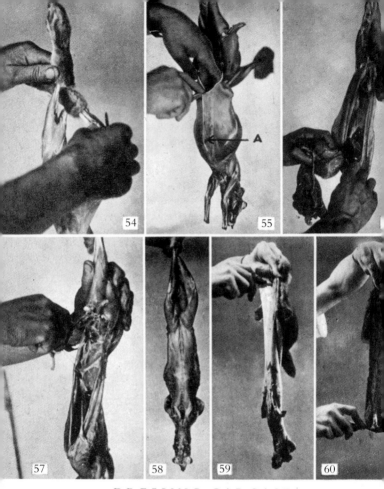

DRESSING CARCASE

54. Cut insertion at hind leg. Thread other leg through at rear.

55. Put two fingers in space made at pelvis. Pulling skin from entrails. Cut down to Mark A.

56. Take out all entrails in one movement. Cutting to release at liver.

57. Taking out gut at pelvis joint.

58. Carcase finished in 'Ostend Fashion.' Note front paws threaded into side.

DIVIDING SKIN

59. Cutting down skin. Starting at vent.

60. Cutting down to lip. Using knife saw fashion.

nest until the 30th day, when they will be quite dry and very lively.

They should be transferred to a very roomy coop with the hen.

See that the floor (loose) fits securely and is covered with a sprinkling of sand or earth. Shut the hen in with the ducklings in darkness to start with, and this is a good practice when ducklings are introduced to a hen for the first time as she may regard them with suspicion.

DUCKLINGS Require well Ventilated Roomy Coops

Shade and Shelter to resort to.

A fountain of clean water deep enough to allow them to dip their heads;

Mash fed moist, but not "sloppy."

Briff Jackson

The feeding can be of crumbly mash as for chicks, fed three or four times daily. Do not give a deep bath. A shallow dish in which they can completely cover their bills is all that is required. But if the receptacle is deep put in some stones.

The ideal hatching date to obtain autumn eggs is April 20, but May ducklings do very well.

If day old ducklings are bought – which is by far the best

way of starting for the beginner – they can later be reared
under a hen or under a Pyramid hover, such as is described
and illustrated under 'Chick Rearing'.

The advantage of the Pyramid or Circular metal hover
over box designs is that more air can quickly be introduced
by removing the curtains and raising the legs and a hurricane lamp often provides sufficient heat for the first ten days.

Care must be taken that the temperature does not rise
above 90° and that the litter (such as peat moss) is quite
dry and changed frequently under the hover.

Since there is no hen to teach the artificially reared duckling how to feed, a little crumbly mash should be sprinkled
on a board or piece of cardboard, or a little fine stale bread-
crumbs sprinkled in the water trough.

In warm weather ducklings require very little brooding.
Even under hens it will be noticed how the ducklings at a
few days old prefer to cuddle up in groups outside the coop.
And they are so remarkably active right from the start that
a small run should surround the coop for the first few days.

The only other points to watch during rearing are plenty
of drinking water, shade (an orchard with its filtered sunlight is excellent) and rats. Never, incidentally, let ducklings
have drinking water in which they can swim for the first few
days, as, oddly, they are liable to drown. Put a brick in the
trough.

SEXING

It is not a difficult matter for an expert to identify the sex of ducklings from a day old by the vent method.

Hence if space is limited it is possible to buy day old ducklets with no drakelets.

Later the sexes can be told fairly accurately by the fact that the young ducks make a distinct 'quack' while the drakes can only wheeze. Near maturity the latter develop their curly feathers in the tail, and in the case of Khaki Campbells their glossy green heads.

DISEASES

Unlike some strains of hens, ducks are remarkably free from diseases. In fact a sick duck can be counted as a dead duck.

The most common ailment in adult ducks is lameness. There is either a wart or corn on the pad or one of the toes is swollen. It is often attributed to the duck's inexhaustible activity on hard ground.

Pinching out the corn, painting with iodine and isolating in a well-littered pen are the only practical remedies.

Ducklings can suffer from exposure to cold winds, thorough soaking in rain and delay in drying, and lack of fresh air or carbon monoxide poisoning.

These are usually evidenced by some peculiarity in gait, such as unsteadiness, and falling backwards. Sunstroke can also induce the same result, and lack of sufficient water to cover the heads may cause sore eyes.

Leg weakness may be due to lack of sunlight (substituted by cod-liver oil), faulty breeding stock and deficiency in the food. Rubbing the legs is quite useless.

In fact with all duck troubles, as with hens, remedies are seldom effective. It is far better to find out the cause by a post mortem by a skilled poultry pathologist and so take preventive measures.

But diseases need not worry the duck initiate. His only trouble is that he expects unlimited eggs from mongrel ducks.

Or if he has the sense to pay better prices for pedigree layers he fails to recognise that they must be fed well if they are to produce their enormous output in a small pen.

Ducks are creatures of intelligence and temperament. They need absolutely regular attention when they respond nobly.

This will be readily forthcoming from anyone who has come under the spell of ducks and eaten their wonderful product. Those who have eaten a *new laid* duck egg know how base is the rumour that a duck egg 'tastes strong'.

GEESE

No birds grow quicker on less supplied food than the goose.

Goslings will weigh over 6 lb. at 8 weeks and at 16 weeks – which is an economic age to kill them – they will weigh over 10 lb.

After 6 weeks they can subsist entirely on grass.

There must, however, be an abundance of short pasture and, in periods of drought, they need steamed potatoes and weatings, and these supplements also help during the final fortnight before killing.

If killed straight off the run without any supplied food they are inclined to be poor in flesh.

Equipment required then is also negligible. After weaning, at a fortnight, they need no housing, and low wire netting will confine them in areas free from foxes.

In view of these advantages, it may be wondered why they are not more widely kept. In war, stocks would undoubtedly increase rapidly because their flesh is succulent and rich in fat.

But the goose population was greatly depleted in peace time for three main reasons:

Goose meat was out of favour because of its richness compared with turkey and cockerel, and fetched an uneconomic price.

Only 4 or 5 goose eggs can be hatched under one hen.

The goose herself does not make a satisfactory mother and incubators have not proved successful. If they were, the gosling would undoubtedly become a profitable proposition,

But although most of the eggs hatch under hens, it needs a large number of broodies to rear any head of stock.

The final failing is that whilst the goose is employed as a 'flying flock' on some farms, where it keeps down the grass, provided it has not become too coarse and tufty, it is also an opportunist.

It will dabble its mischievous and muddy bill in every water and food trough that it can find. Its droppings, moreover, are liable to become too overwhelming for any small area.

It is a bird which is in its element in orchards or paddocks. or even lawns, which would not otherwise be occupied with other stock.

Given reasonably short turf to start with, the goose has a remarkable effect in encouraging the finer grasses.

The principal breeds of geese are: Embden (White), Toulouse (Grey), Roman (White), Brecon Buff, Chinese (Grey and White).

The Embden and Toulouse are the largest breeds and the cross between the two makes the best table birds. The Roman is a good commercial goose and the Brecon Buff is a hardy small goose with plenty of breast meat.

The Chinese is a very pretty goose, rather noisy, the best layer of all the geese but not so good for table.

The Toulouse and Embden breeds will lay up to 40 eggs in a season and Chinese up to 60, and they start laying in mid-February.

A breeding pen consists of one gander to three or four

geese, and they can be bred from for ten or twelve years, or even longer.

They prefer swimming water, but it is by no means essential for fertility. Some deep bath or pool in which they can wash themselves is advisable.

The eggs should be set under hens, two being set at a time, on 4 to 5 eggs. Incubation takes 28 to 30 days and the treatment of the hens should be the same as for brooding chicks, except that the turf under the eggs should be kept moister and the eggs should be turned each day by hand.

The floor of the coop in which the hen and goslings are placed after hatching should be well covered with sand, as a slippery surface causes sprawly legs.

Some breeders use sacks as a floor, but the bare earth is not recommended in case of raids by rats.

If two lots of goslings are placed under one hen, the coop wants to be roomy, as goslings grow with incredible rapidity.

Young goslings are a little shy of food to start with, but they can be fed the same as chicks with a rather larger allowance of minced green food.

After the first fortnight, they require no brooding and the number of meals can be gradually reduced so that by the end of the month they have only three.

They should then be gradually weaned on to grass and chopped green food.

Their water fountain should allow them to immerse their heads and not their bodies, and a tongue glass serves the purpose well.

A beginner might well start with day-old goslings, and if he had no broody, use a brooder of one of the types mentioned in a previous chapter. As an alternative, in the summer a hurricane lamp in a house will suffice.

They can be killed at any age from 16 weeks, when they will weigh from 10 lb. upwards.

It is extremely difficult to tell the sex, even in mature geese, except by the vent method.

Goose feathers, especially from White geese, fetch very good prices from reputable merchants.

KEEPING RABBITS ON SCRAPS

By Claude H. Goodchild

—

At no time in our history, has this country been placed in such a critical position for the future supplies of all foods.

It is therefore of the greatest importance for everyone to 'pull their weight' and utilise their spare time to the best advantage.

Many are now producing their own vegetables, but for the heavy manual worker, meat is an essential.

The production of rabbit flesh is the most economical means of bridging our present meat difficulty.

The reason is explained by the following:

Rabbits can be fed in spare time on food which would otherwise be waste, and are ready for table at 4 months old.

Immediate results can therefore be forthcoming, and increased yields can be obtained at an amazing rate if the information can be conveyed to all who are willing and in a position to participate.

When Soviet Russia was short of meat, their Government imported large numbers of breeding stock in rabbits, chiefly from Great Britain, and quickly worked up regular supplies of rabbit meat for their workers.

Before the commencement of the recent war Germany promoted large schemes for the production of millions of rabbits. Italy passed a decree making it compulsory when practical for everyone to keep rabbits. It is unfortunate having to introduce this section with comparisons, but they are facts which need no further comment.

The aim of this book is to give practical guidance in as simple a form as possible, catering for the needs of the breeder who intends starting with a small number of rabbits, and no previous knowledge – not the large commercial rabbit farmer, but no doubt many who start now will remain in the commercial ranks of the rabbit industry.

Information given is based on 25 years' practical experience and will, it is hoped, be of interest and use to all who can be 'rabbit minded'.

The rabbit industry varies considerably from other trades in the respect that a newcomer can become expert in a very short time, and although there is always something new to learn, novices can often teach the old lag quite a lot. The newcomer to rabbit breeding must have initiative, be a lover of animals, and prepared to learn if he wishes to climb high on the ladder of fame.

Practical knowledge is of the highest importance; far too many publications have in the past been compiled with too much leaning to the theoretical side, which has a dangerous tendency, unless the knowledge is absorbed by one who has practical knowledge, and for that reason references to statistics and theory are avoided as far as possible.

Many authors, lacking practical experience, confine the bulk of their masterpiece to laborious details of some scientific discovery on which they themselves are the only authority, and leave the reader confused and doubtful as to his ability in starting.

Soak the mind of the beginner in practical hints, in a form which can easily be again referred to and success is certain. Later he can with his own discretion use the knowledge gained by scientific research.

This publication has been compiled with the intention that all the novices' practical queries should have their answers clearly shown. The impossible cannot be achieved, but it is hoped that sufficient knowledge is imparted to enable many rabbit breeders to start up with successful results and join in the pleasures of a hobby and business combined.

Finally, I must place on record my appreciation of the assistance given to me by Mr Alan Thompson, Editor *Poultry Farmer*, both in the compilation of these pages and in his photographs which illustrate them.

All details given are the direct result of practical experience, and no information has been taken from other writings. Far too many books are compiled by unpractical authors, weaving together parts from books of other 'authorities'.

OFFICIAL RABBIT RATIONS

Bran is the only food – apart from that which was home grown – that was allowed by the Government to rabbit-keepers in wartime.

It can be obtained by applying for registration to the Ministry of Agriculture, Rationing Division, Hotel Glendower, Lytham St. Annes, Lancs., marking the envelope 'Rabbits' and stating the number of breeding does kept.

Those with four does and under can only get the bran ration – which is 7 lb. of bran per quarter for each doe – through a Domestic Rabbit Club. Only one ration is allowed for each household.

Those with 5, 6 or 7 does are treated as domestic producers with 4 does and receive their bran ration through a Rabbit Club only (28 lb. per quarter).

The minimum membership for such a Club is normally 12.

For details of Club formation, especially in isolated districts, get into touch with the Area Organiser, c/o the Domestic Poultry Keepers' Council, 55 Whitehall, London, SW1.

Those with eight does and over are regarded as commercial rabbit producers and can obtain their rations – 7 lb. per doe per quarter – without the necessity of joining any Club, by applying for registration to the Ministry of Agriculture,

Rationing Division, Hotel Glendower, Lytham St. Annes, Lancs.

Their rations will, however, only be issued in complete units of four does. Thus a rabbit keeper with 11 or 14 does receives rations for only 8 or 12 does respectively.

Wire netting is unrationed. If in difficulty, apply to your local Area Organiser, who will put you in touch with suppliers.

RABBIT MEAT FROM SCRAPS
VARIETY TO HAVE

The first question which arises when starting rabbit breeding, is which is the best variety.

There is no best variety, but some are more suited for the purpose you have in mind, and much depends on personal preference.

There are a great many varieties which fill the present-day needs for meat production, and for the novice it is advisable to make their selection from one of the following crosses: Flemish–Belgian, Flemish–English and Flemish–Dutch.

These varieties have been found for a number of years to be the most suitable, being very prolific and hardy, the progeny mature quickly and produce the best carcase.

These varieties were most commonly used in Belgium and Holland for the Ostend carcase trade. There are quantities of stock in these varieties for sale at moderate prices.

The Dutch produces an excellent carcase. Although a small variety, they mature quickly and are very hardy and keep in the best of condition with the minimum of feeding. An admirable variety where accommodation is limited: ideal for the backyarder with limited space.

Most fur varieties are very suitable for meat and fur production, and give breeders additional returns from the skin value which is considerable.

To get the best value from the skins the rabbits have to be run on for a longer period than with the ordinary meat rabbit.

At present it is policy to advise breeders to start with table rabbits.

There is a very limited quantity of breeding stock available in the fur varieties. Owing to the great national necessity to get as many fresh rabbit breeders started as soon as possible, it is best to leave the breeding of the fur varieties in the hands of the more experienced, who can handle the skins to the best advantage.

Later when stock in the fur varieties is more plentiful it will be a good plan to add some to your existing stock of table rabbits, when you will have gained much valuable experience in the general management.

To create a sudden big demand for stock in the fur varieties would tend to push prices to a very high level.

PURCHASING STOCK

Having decided on the variety or type of rabbit to start with, the question of purchasing arises. See Varieties of Rabbits.

There are rabbit, smallholding and poultry publications which have reliable advertisers. Buy from an experienced breeder. If you have any doubts, utilise the deposit system of the paper from which you took the advertisement. The Area Organisers of the Domestic Poultry Keepers' Council (55 Whitehall, SW1) will assist in putting you in touch with reliable breeders.

NUMBER TO START WITH

The number of breeding does to start with must depend on your aims. For personal household use, it is advisable to start with a minimum of 3 does and 1 buck. (*See further details under Stud Buck.*)

BREEDING AGE

The satisfactory age at which a doe can be bred from, depends on how it is matured. Most varieties will conceive at 4 to 5 months. It is dangerous to breed from immatured stock. They will not mature later, prove bad mothers, and produce valueless progeny. In summer months maturity can be at 6 months, in the winter 7 months – much depends on growth.

Best results are obtained by starting with stock at least 8 months of age. Does are liable to neglect their first litters, especially in the autumn and winter.

Usually this defect does not re-occur. This may be due to moult, lack of sunshine, and suitable foods to stimulate a flush of milk. Experienced mothers are the best to breed from during the more difficult period, mated to a young, vigorous buck.

QUALITY OF BREEDERS

It is essential to start with the best quality healthy stock. On no account breed from a deformed or unhealthy rabbit. Chief indications of a healthy rabbit are, shiny smooth coat, alert eye, clean nose, dung in firm pellets.

HANDLING

A rabbit should be lifted by supporting the hind quarters with the left hand and gripping the ears and fur at nape of neck with the right (*see Plate* 44). Avoid handling doe in kindle, especially just before the due date.

STUD BUCK

The buck or bucks used for mating the does should be of the best quality. Extra care and good regular feeding is necessary. The buck imparts health and strength to the litter, especially in the early stages. Never breed from a buck which is out of sorts. A stud buck should not be allowed more than 5 matings per week.

MATING

There is no definite period when a rabbit is in season. It varies with the time of the year and condition of the rabbit. In the spring, does are practically always ready to mate, whereas at other times of the year it may take several days to gain success. Matings in winter are best obtained in warmer days. Place the doe in the buck's hutch, when one of four things will happen.

1. The doe sits hunched up and ignores buck.
2. The doe chases round the hutch in playful manner.
3. The doe whines or goes for the buck.
4. The doe remains still, arches her back and makes things easier for the buck.

In cases 1 and 3 remove doe and try again later. 2. Wait a few minutes and case 4 may occur. 4. Successful mating is almost a certainty.

The completion of the act is shown by the buck falling over on its side with ears back with or without crying out.

A scream is thought by beginners to indicate hurt to the doe. This is not so but perfect mating.

Sometimes a buck will do this part without effecting an entry.

If this is suspected, examine that part of the doe for signs of the conception. It is not always necessary for visible satisfactory matings to be successful, and it is advisable to place the doe in with the buck again on the 14th day.

An expert can tell at this period by hand handling if the doe is in kindle. A beginner should not try this. Damage can be caused by rough handling.

GESTATION PERIOD

A litter is produced 31 days after mating.

MATED DOES

Does can be purchased ready mated, but it is advisable to
have a buck or one within easy reach for future mating.
Avoid sending for mating by rail. There is so much loss of
time and expense, and the journey tends to increase the
risk of unsuccessful mating.

KINDLING

Does are usually very restless several days before the litter
appears. To avoid disturbance during this period, thoroughly clean the hutch out one week before kindling date,
and give a liberal supply of litter in the hutch. Usually this
is all heaped in a corner quite a time before the litter
arrives.

Does often go off their feed just prior to kindling. Remove
any stale food and give fresh. Fresh water is essential.

ARRIVAL OF LITTER

Although does have usually made a large heap of litter in
the darkest corner of the hutch for the expected family, they
usually produce the litter before completing the final act
of pulling quantities of fur from their flanks and back to
keep the young absolutely warm.

Some careless mothers produce their litter scattered all
over the hutch floor, and in the cold weather they will be
dead in a very short time. This neglect is unaccountable
and usually does not recur.

If this is noticed in time, put all young together in a nest surrounded with warm fine hay. The mother will later do the rest. (*See section referring to Mothers eating young.*)

SIZE OF LITTER

The number of young in a litter varies considerably. Anything from 1 to 14. An average litter is 5 to 7.

It is always advisable to examine the young as soon as born – removing any dead in nest, if left they may all die. If litter is too large kill off surplus, allowing the strongest babies to live.

The number to leave depends on the capabilities of the mother which are regulated by the time of the year and quality of food. From January up to the end of July, 6 to 7 is a good litter to leave, in the other period 5 to 6.

FOSTERING

If you have a doe of special merit and prize the progeny, mate another doe the same day as her and assuming the litter of your special doe is of average size or over, kill off the young of the other doe, and put half the young of the special doe to this doe which is now termed a foster-mother doe. Before doing this operation, take note of the following instructions:

1. Take both does concerned out and feed.
2. Make sure your hands smell correctly by rubbing fingers in litter of hutch concerned before handling young.
3. Take away all foster-mother's young — don't mix.
4. The young which are put into the foster's nest can be made to smell correctly by sprinkling with litter from foster's hutch.
5. Feed does with 'tit bits' as soon as put back to distract attention.

6. Disturb nests as little as possible, and make sure there is no fur on the young when transferring.

Fostering can be done up to 4 days, but the safest time is between 12 and 24 hours after birth. A difference of age between the young of the doe and foster of more than 2 days makes it tricky. The quality of the milk changes after the birth of the young.

WEANING

The age at which a rabbit can be weaned depends on the time of the year and growth. When food is plentiful and good, weaning can be done at 4 to 5 weeks, in autumn and winter 6 to 7 weeks. Great care in careful feeding should be exercised when young are first weaned. Give only the best food (as described later) and feed often.

If allowed to get hungry they are liable to over-gorge at their next meal and develop indigestion and scours.

It is advisable when possible to wean young into runs or colonies with several in a place where there is room for exercise.

RECORDS

It is advisable to keep full records of all stock intended for breeding. A system should be adopted to keep a trace of the breeding stock. If kept in single hutches a hutch card is all that is necessary.

The difficulty arises when mixing litters together, when some form of individual marking is necessary to keep trace.

TATTOOING

Tattooing is simple and most effective, and if done with care is lasting. Place the rabbit's ear flat on a piece of soft wood and with a large-sized needle dipped in marking ink, prick out the number or marking required.

After the operation, smear over with the ink.

Another method is to ring the stock. Special rings are supplied for this purpose. These are put on by slipping over the hind foot up to the hock. These are made in different sizes for each variety by the British Rabbit Council, 273, Farnborough Road, Farnborough, Hants.

BREEDING PERIOD

Tame rabbits breed freely throughout the year, but the output from a doe should be limited to 4 litters per year. It is not advantageous to go beyond that, or it will effect the health of the doe and render it unable to rear litters until it has a complete rest.

TABLE SHOWING STEADY BREEDING WITHOUT UNDUE STRAIN ON THE DOE

Mate	Born	Wean	Kill Youngsters
January	February	April	June to July
April	May	July	September to October
July	August	October	December to January
October	November	January	March to April

The output can be compared to a motor – good petrol and oil, and steady driving gives lasting wear. Given good food and steady breeding the doe will last for several seasons. Abuse of this rule means complete breakdown.

A doe will remain good for breeding for an average of 4 seasons, but is usually replaced before that time by one of better quality.

INBREEDING

The extent to which the breeding of relations together can be conducted depends entirely on the stamina and type of rabbit.

For table purposes avoid inbreeding; it serves no good

purpose. For exhibition stock inbreeding is necessary, but should be done very carefully.

Often certain outstanding qualities are only contained in certain closely related rabbits, and to improve the standard of the strain, the mating of close relations is necessary. Having done this once, the progeny should be mated to almost unrelated stock.

Disastrous results can be obtained by inbreeding at random. To be successful it is necessary to keep a strict record of the breeders and make full observations at all stages and avoid breeding from any stock which is lacking in stamina and vitality.

HAND REARING

It happens that a doe may die possibly from the effects of kindling or other defects, and usually breeders, chiefly out of sympathy, consider they can rear the young with a fountain pen filler and cow's milk.

It is not worth the trouble, even if they are valuable youngsters. Chances of success are too remote. If attempted, dilute cow's milk with 25 per cent to 50 per cent water, and feed morning and night. Avoid over-feeding. Snag – change of food causes indigestion, diarrhœa and death.

SEXING

The earliest stage when youngsters can be safely sexed is at 4 weeks. Great care should be taken in this operation. Avoid undue forcing in order to expose the organ.

Hold the rabbit by placing your thumb and index finger of your right hand at base of ears and the palm of your hand at back of the head, allow the rump of the rabbit to rest limply between your legs, then press the organ with thumb and first finger of the left hand. The male organ protrudes in a cylinder shape and the female only protrudes one side in a triangular shape. (*See Plate* 45.)

CASTRATION

Castration is very seldom done on rabbits. It has very few advantages. The chief reason is to prevent bucks from fighting in colonies. For table purposes only, bucks are killed before they reach that stage. For fur it has the effect of making the rabbit lazy and retards the fur growth. Castrated rabbits never appear in prime fur. For these reasons there is no object in describing this skilled operation.

EXHIBITING

This country stands foremost in the world for exhibition stock of the highest quality. If breeders abroad need the best quality stock or stock to improve their own, they have to buy in England. In normal times there has always been a good export market. The chief reasons for the outstanding quality of rabbits in this country are:

(*a*) Large numbers of Shows in easy reach of all breeders.
(*b*) The right quality of foods produced in the British Isles combined with the ideal climate.

The soil in this country contains minerals which are highly beneficial for the outstanding qualities of our stock. This is a very serious disadvantage to breeders in other countries.

(*c*) The outstanding sportsmanship of the British community, who appreciate honour and are not disheartened by defeat.

Successful breeders of exhibition stock are well rewarded. There is always a good demand for prize-winning stock at very satisfactory prices. A champion rabbit in most varieties is worth anything from £50 upwards.

Before starting in exhibition breeding, visit some shows and see the judging and acquaint yourself with the different varieties and the points to aim at, then purchase good quality stock from a breeder of repute. It is not always the best which produce the best, so get advice or put yourself in the breeder's hands.

Show your stock as soon as possible, compare yours with others and don't expect prize cards right away. There are lots of interesting things to learn. A visit to a show is a grand way of combining business with pleasure.

Having decided on the variety or varieties to take up, join the specialist club for the breed, also the British Rabbit Council, and ring your stock. Ringing enables you to compete for all specials offered. Also join the nearest Rabbit Fanciers' Club, which can inform you fully regarding shows.

JUDGING

Judging of live stock is only an expert's task, usually backed by a life experience. The chief points, as a percentage basis of awards, are laid down by the Specialist Club for the variety in question. To the inexperienced these points should only be taken as guidance, giving stress to the outstanding requirements of the breed.

In practice, an exhibit will be discarded for a slight fault, such as a white spot on nose or foot. One of the most important points which the judge is bound to notice with stock of equal merit and which may sway his views, is general condition. Primary importance is given to condition, health, correct size, colour and shape without noticeable faults.

FERTILITY AND STERILITY

It seldom happens that a rabbit cannot breed. Sterility is usually external and caused by fighting, especially with the male. It occasionally happens that rabbits are born without the organs being correctly formed.

When sterility is suspected it is frequently temporary and brought about by the female condition.

There is a natural breeding season for the wild rabbit, which is from December up to July, and the tame rabbit is most fertile during this period.

Matings from August up to December are more difficult. Lack of sunshine and corresponding falling-off in feeding value in green food at this period plays an important part. Matings then are most successful on warm days.

Many matings with stock of the highest vitality may prove unsuccessful. To improve fertility, feed with fresh green food, and for stubborn cases try food rich in protein: maple peas soaked 24 hours before feeding and sprouted oats.

RABBIT MANURE

Rabbit manure is a valuable product, and is rich in nitrogen, phosphoric acid and potash. It can be used fresh or rotted. It is suitable for all types of garden crops, especially greens.

Avoid using sawdust abundant in turpentine. This has injurious effects and promotes fungus. Much wrong advice is given on this product by farmers, who are under the wrong impression that where wild rabbits feed, nothing will grow. The fact is, rabbits eat off corn when it first comes up. At that stage it dies from bleeding. When rabbits run on young corn when there is a frost followed by the sun these patches scorch and die. Years of results have shown that rabbit manure is more productive than other farm-yard manure.

VARIETIES OF RABBITS

To describe the different breeds of rabbits in detail would

SOME POPULAR VARIETIES OF RABBITS AND THEIR USES

	Variety	Colour	Meat Quality	Fur Quality	Adult Weight	Chief Uses
TABLE VARIETIES	Belgian Hare	Rufous red	Good	Mixed tames for dyeing	8 lb.	Pure and crossed for meat
	Checkered Giant	Black, blue and grey, spotted on white basis	Good	Mixed tames for dyeing	Over 9 lb.	Pure and crossed for meat
	Dutch	Black, blue, steel, tortoiseshell and yellow	Small and good	Mixed tames for dyeing	5½ lb.	Pure and chiefly for crossing for meat
	Flemish Giant	Dark steel, black and slate	Good	Mixed tames for dyeing	Over 11 lb.	Pure and crossed for meat
	Lop	Black, grey and sooty fawn	Medium	Mixed tames for dyeing	8–10 lb.	Meat and scientific research
	Silvers	Brown, black and fawn	Small and good	Fair	6 lb.	Meat and fur
	English	Black, blue, steel, fawn and tortoiseshell	Good	Mixed tames for dyeing	6–8 lb.	Pure and crossed for meat
NORMAL FUR VARIETIES	Argente Beverens	White, brown and blue	Medium	Medium	5–7 lb.	Meat and fur
		Black-blue, brown and white	Good	Good	Over 7 lb.	Fur and meat
	Chinchilla	Blue-grey	Good	Very good	5½–6½ lb.	Fur and meat
	Chinchilla Giganta	Blue-grey	Good	Very good	Up to 11 lb.	Fur and meat
	Havana	Rich chocolate	Small and good	Very good	6 lb.	Fur and meat

Variety	Colour	Meat Quality	Fur Quality	Adult Weight	Chief Uses
NORMAL FUR VARIETIES					
Lilac	Pinky dove	Small and good	Medium	6 lb.	Fur and meat
Sable (Marten and Siamese)	Sepia, brown	Good	Very good	5–7 lb.	Fur and meat
Silver Fox ..	Black ticked white hairs	Good	Medium	5–7 lb.	Fur and meat
Siberians	Black, brown, blue	Good	Good	6 lb.	Fur and meat
REX FUR VARIETIES					
Bluerex :	Medium slate	Good	Excellent	5–7 lb.	Fur and meat
Chinchillarex :	Blue-grey	Good	Excellent	5–7 lb.	Fur and meat
Erminerex :	White	Good	Good	5–7 lb.	Fur and meat
Havanarex :	Beaver brown	Good	Excellent	5–7 lb.	Fur and meat
Lilacrex :	Pinky dove	Good	Excellent	5–7 lb.	Fur and meat
Lynxrex :	Golden fawn silvered	Good	Excellent	5–7 lb.	Fur and meat
Sablerex (Siamese and Marten) :	Sepia brown	Good	Excellent	5–7 lb.	Fur and meat
Nutriarex ..	Light shade of beaver	Good	Excellen	5–7 lb.	Fur and meat
Sealrex ..	Brownish black	Good	Excellent	5–7 lb.	Fur and meat
Angora ..	White and various colours	Poor	For wool	Over 5 lb.	Wool production

The above details are intended to assist novices when making their choice for breeding for utility purposes. The list does not include all varieties, but those considered the most useful. Readers wishing to obtain a full list of recognised breeds of rabbits, and standards for exhibition, should join the British Rabbit Council, which issues a book to all members giving full information relating to each variety.

take more space than the total size of this book, and prove
most confusing to the novice.

Although there are a great number of different varieties
of rabbits, there are many of equal merit and importance
which serve the same purpose, i.e. meat and/or fur.

For the purpose of this book and the intentions for which
it is written, the varieties are generalised under headings for
which those particular types are most suited for utility
purposes.

There are three chief reasons for breeding rabbits for
commercial purposes: (a) meat, (b) fur, (c) wool, and there
are many varieties equally suited for one or two of these
requirements.

All varieties are used for exhibition purposes, and have
their specialist Clubs, which lay down the standards for
that breed and give specials to members of the club exhibit-
ing at Shows supported by that particular club.

The health and stamina of the different varieties of
rabbits depend mainly on how the stock has been bred and
managed. All varieties, if properly managed and bred, are
equal in health and stamina.

The larger sized rabbits, such as Flemish Giants, need
more care and attention up to maturity.

Specialise in breeding from stock which has given the best
results. Some does are much better mothers than others.

Try to record mothers which supply abundance of milk
and work up a strain built up from good milk-recorded
stock. Many rabbitries have neglected this most important
fact, and have concentrated more on the type of stock they
are producing, and maybe bred from a succession of bad
mothers, yielding small milk supplies insufficient to rear a
reasonable size litter satisfactorily.

When breeding the fur varieties, the chief points to aim
at are colour, even, clear and rich, good density of fur, and
nice silky texture. Coarse, rough-coated rabbits are unsuited

for the furriers' needs. Uneven colour and pale colouring generally means that the skins are used for dyeing purposes, and are not of the same value.

Skins of the natural fur varieties of rabbits are manufactured in their natural condition. The colours do not fade to the same extent as dyed skins, and retain their beauty.

Lower quality skins, and wild rabbit skins are dyed for furriers' purposes.

Some dyed skins are the cause of dermatitis (eruption of the skin); this adds to the value of the undyed skins.

Coats made from good quality Rex rabbits were retailing at £40 before the recent war, and in big demand.

Readers should note that all articles made from dyed rabbit skins are marketed as Coney, with various prefixes in an attempt to delude the public into the belief that they are the genuine furs to which they refer. Thus, Beaver Coney, and Squirrel Coney.

There are breeds and crosses of rabbits bred entirely for meat production, and of course rabbits bred for meat and fur purposes, each suitably filling the requirements. It would be wrong not to mention the fur varieties under this title, because as meat producers they can claim merits of the highest standard.

Usually breeders of the fur varieties aim at producing skins of the highest value and take the meat side of the production as a secondary consideration.

There are also breeders whose aims are chiefly meat and secondly skins. To meet this requirement the fur rabbit is again required.

For the purpose of this book it is considered best to explain at a glance by means of the chart on a foregoing page the chief characteristics of the different varieties, and not to confuse the reader's mind with a long description and details of every variety, but mention only a few of the most important and useful to fulfil the present-day needs.

MEAT VARIETIES

For the sole purpose of meat production, varieties such as Flemish Giants, Chequered Giants, Belgian Hares, Dutch and Silvers are used most often, and generally crossed to improve the stamina and to promote rapid growth. When crossed they intermix the good points for meat production and increase the vitality.

These varieties have been bred for generations for table production and for this sole purpose are hard to better. They were the chief breeds kept in Belgium and Holland to cater for the needs of the British market. Skins of all these varieties have a considerable value and should be carefully handled.

Practically all the medium quality Coney coats and fur-backed gloves were produced from this type of rabbit in Europe. They were dressed, machined and dyed and forwarded to England for manufacture. *It is to be hoped that in the very near future, this country will be in a position, in addition to exporting quantities, to supply a great proportion of its own needs.*

NORMAL FUR VARIETIES

From 1918 onwards, there was a great shortage of all furs, due to conditions brought about by the First World War and increased popularity for wear due to rapid increase in the standard of living at that period.

This resulted in the prices of all rabbit skins reaching a very high level and influenced breeders to undertake many experiments to create and stabilise new varieties of rabbits which produced suitable skins for the fur trade.

This resulted in many breeds of rabbits being produced which yielded skins of delicate shades of colour and fine texture. This was the foundation of a now firmly established industry which has played a big part in fulfilling the needs of the rapid expansion of the fur trade.

The chief difference in the skins of these fur varieties from the ordinary type previously produced, is the colour and improvement in texture. The general character has not been altered, consequently the general term NORMAL FUR VARIETIES was adopted.

The chief and most valuable of these varieties are CHIN-CHILLAS, HAVANA, BEVERENS and SABLES. They are old-established breeds, and there is always a good demand for the skins. In addition, they produce carcases of the highest quality and are ideal 'dual purpose' (fur and meat) varieties.

They are exceptionally hardy and prolific. Bucks of these varieties are used extensively for crossing with table varieties for meat production. It means an entire out cross for the table varieties and promotes vigour and quick maturity.

REX FUR VARIETIES

The breeding of the normal fur varieties was taken up on a large scale by commercial rabbit breeders, with very satisfactory results, and up to the outbreak of the 1939 war, many thousands of these skins were used in London. It is regrettable to state that a very large percentage were imported owing to cheaper cost of production abroad and lack of interest in this country.

By pure chance at a time when the utmost interests were concerned in the production of skins from the normal fur varieties in many countries, an entirely different type of rabbit turned up. This was first 'spotted' in France.

This new type of fur rabbit was later known as the Castorrex, and possessed entirely different characteristics to the normal fur varieties. The fur is devoid of all guard hairs with no whiskers. It is plush-like in appearance, very dense and gives the same appearance, only much better, than the best skins of the normal fur varieties which had been pulled.

Pulling is a term used for taking off the guard hairs and leaving a clear plush effect.

The original of these varieties as previously stated was the Castorrex, which was a wild grey rabbit colour.

Breeders immediately realised that confined to this colour the prospects for skins would be limited, and proceeded with the valuable and infallible aid of Mendel's theory of breeding to produce nearly every variety of rabbit with these particular characteristics.

This was known as 'Rexing' the different varieties, and each variety so 'Rexed' had the suffix Rex added to its title.

The origin or intention of the word REX is obscure, but a more suitable descriptive word could not have been used if taken literally to imply the king of fur varieties.

The skins in comparison to other varieties are outstanding and of much greater value.

The time will come when the furs will be known to all and considered the aristocrat, or king, of the rabbit species.

The chief characteristics of the skins of these varieties are the delicate and lasting colours, superb density and softness, in fact such a softness as no other fur possesses, and a most marvellous plush-like appearance, giving lasting wear and *no* shedding of fur.

Some skins are so near to perfection that many noted furriers cannot tell what species they are or even if they are rabbit.

The chart of Popular Varieties of Rabbits gives a few of the most popular of the Rex varieties.

For breeding for commercial purposes it is advisable to make the selection to start with from one of these varieties.

Matching is difficult unless there is a good selection of skins to choose from. These varieties also produce ideal carcasses for the meat trade.

It is important to remember that the Rex was originally produced by successive inbreeding. In the early stages stamina was greatly lacking and needed a lot of outbreeding to counteract, and with the very limited number of this breed in existence, the task was slow.

For several years the stamina has been brought to normal and the health of the breed is now up to average and compares most favourably with all other varieties; in fact Rex are now noted for being excellent mothers and rear large litters. For several years they have been bred and reared outside in a similar fashion to the hardiest of rabbits.

In view of the foregoing, it is advisable to exercise every discretion when inbreeding to any extent. Continual inbreeding with these varieties has the tendency to revert to degenerate characteristics and severely damage health. The actual origin of the original Rex is known to be degenerate resulting from line breeding. However, that is now history.

ANGORA

The Angora rabbit has already been referred to under the heading of WOOL. As the breed is only used for wool production, and not for meat, it is not within the scope covered by the title of this book.

HOUSING OF RABBITS
HUTCHES

It is most difficult to advise on definite methods of housing rabbits, as so much depends on what materials are available.

For small domestic breeders, unless money is no object, make your own. It is not necessary to have any previous experience of carpentering.

The following hints and accompanying diagrams should enable you to produce a very satisfactory result. For many generations, cottage people have kept rabbits with every success in what would now be termed most unsuitable conditions, and frequently a doe and 8 youngsters have thrived in a hutch 18 in. by 12 in., literally sitting on top of each other, with cleaning out operations unknown. To add to the discomfort this equipment was often placed in a damp cellar without any ventilation.

This is mentioned to show that rabbits are hardy and can be made to thrive in most difficult circumstances.

Before deciding on the type of hutch to make, arrange where to keep the rabbits.

For the small householder with a small space, the choice is limited, and usually the breeding does are hutched in a small outhouse, with additional running-on hutches beside the garden wall or fence.

When planning this make sure that the shed is well ventilated and the outside site, if walled in, is not too hot.

It is a mistake to place hutches facing the sun in the summer months; the heat inside would be terrific. In the winter and early spring sun is beneficial to all ages.

If a brick wall or other similar type of fence divides the garden, a good plan is to place the hutches back to this, with a roof, covering the hutches, similar to the photograph reproduced in this book. (*See Plate* 46.)

It is always advisable to make hutches in separate units. Hutches built into the side of a shed, using the shed as part of the hutch, are unsuitable.

Hutches made in this way are difficult to clean, and it is difficult to keep rats out.

Also rabbits will gnaw any protruding edges and may seriously damage the building.

Separate units if stood a few inches away from the side of a building should be safe from rats.

For that reason keep the top of the hutch and floor clear of rubbish. Rats usually work from concealed places.

There are various ways and methods of keeping rabbits, depending on the ultimate aim, and facilities at hand.

For the ordinary small breeder whose interest is mainly

to grow a few rabbits for home consumption, only a small equipment and a moderate outlay is necessary.

For the beginner starting with 3 does and 1 buck, the first outlay should be for 1 stack of 3 compartments breeding hutches, and 1 single buck hutch. Plates 42 and 43 show suitable hutches for the purpose and sketches show how to make them.

The next step is to make provision for the increase in stock.

Note that each mother should be having a litter which should average 6 youngsters for weaning every 10 to 12 weeks. See diagram of annual output for a doe on page 109.

Assuming that the progeny will be killed for table at 4 to 5 months old, giving the producer 1 to 2 rabbits per week for his table, accommodation will be required for 4 litters of different ages at the same time (assuming does are mated at different stages).

It is not advisable to run rabbits of vastly different ages together.

Consequently for this purpose, it is advisable to use either the following: Morant type, see Fig. 32, Weaning type, see growing-on type, Plate 43, also Plate 46, and for the larger breeder the colony system, see Figs. 33 and 33a, pages 131–132. Further details of these types are given later.

Many breeders retard the progress of their stock by not making provision in advance and leaving the litters over-crowded with the mother.

This may cause permanent damage to the health of the youngsters. Any check with young growing stock is difficult to put right, and deaths at a later stage may be attributed to other faults. Also, running with the mother too long lessens the annual output from the breeding doe.

Remember when constructing a hutch that it is a lasting job that is needed, and every attention must be given to make the hutch water-tight. Paint or solignum is the best preservative ·for the outside and tar for the roof. Avoid tarring any part which is handled. In hot weather tar melts and becomes a nuisance.

Ruberoid roofing felt or galvanised corrugated iron are both suitable for roofing. If neither are procurable, a sound roofing can be made by first tarring the surface which it is required to cover, then placing ordinary sacking on, and tar and sand. Half inch mesh wire netting should be used for all doors, in as heavy gauge as possible. Always put the netting inside the door to prevent gnawing. Tools necessary for making hutches: saw, hammer and screwdriver and wirecutters.

When constructing a hutch every attention should be given to labour saving, hygiene and lasting wear. The sketch given overleaf is the result of many years' experiments, and has proved to be the most suitable in every respect for breeding does.

There is a lot of liquid coming from rabbits, and unless this can be cleaned out at frequent intervals the hutches will smell and also be injurious to the stock. The best means to avoid this is to adopt the drainage system as shown on sketch.

This has the advantage of allowing all liquid to drain from the hutch immediately, leaving the floor dry and free from smell.

If the hutch is outside, the drainage can be allowed to drop directly on the ground, if in an inside shed a tin guttering should be used to divert the drainage outside.

It is a saving to make the hutches in stacks of 3, which means that 3 separate hutches are made on the same framing, but having individual doors.

When possible construct hutches with $\frac{1}{2}$ or $\frac{5}{8}$ inch boards, matching for preference, on 2-inch by 1-inch quartering.

The wire netting door should be made of $\frac{1}{2}$-inch or $\frac{3}{4}$-inch

Fig. 27. DRAINAGE SYSTEM FOR HUTCHES
Side elevation of stack hutch 3 tier high

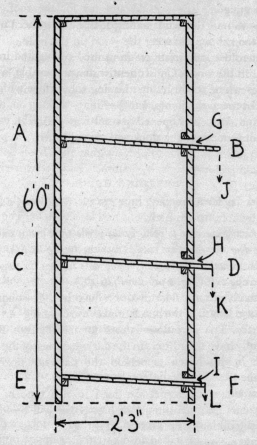

Floors. A to B, C to D, E to F slanting to rear of hutch **allowing a fall of 1½ inches.**

At G, H and I leave an opening 1 inch at rear of hutch to **keep space open for drainage.**

Overlap floors at rear, allowing drainage to drop clear of hutch.

Arrange protrusions as follows:

Distance from back of hutch at **B 3 inches, D 2 inches, F 1 inch.**

Note hutch must be level, to allow dripping at J, K, L to fall clear of hutch.

wire netting of a heavy gauge, as rabbits soon bite through a thin gauge.

Always nail the wire netting inside the door. This prevents the rabbits gnawing the wood on the inside.

Remember that moisture from rain and inside drainage will swell the wood. Consequently allowance must be made for this when constructing the doors by allowing a good space between the joints, $\frac{1}{8}$ to $\frac{1}{4}$ in.

Hutch doors are opened several times each day and if difficult to manage the stock will get neglected.

BREEDING HUTCH

A good size for a breeding hutch is 3 ft. 6 in. long, 2 ft. 3 in. wide by 1 ft. 10 in. high.

By having one door to open for the whole front and a small wire netting door hinged on the outside door opening up half the front, it gives the valuable advantage of being able to open the whole front for cleaning out. (Fig. 27a, also Plate 42.)

Actually it is one door made on the other. The door going the whole length of the hutch, makes the cleaning-out operation easy. The wire door is used for feeding, etc. Rabbits generally have their litters in the darkest corner of the hutch, which in this hutch is behind the part not opened for feeding.

Nest boxes are sometimes used in this type of hutch, particulars and advantages of nest boxes will be found in this book under NEST BOXES (Fig. 34). These kind of hutches are used for inside use; if used for outside they should have a special roofing protection as shown in the photograph of running-on hutches, with roofing. Plate 46.

CONVERTING PACKING CASES

Packing cases are easily converted into suitable hutches.

The sketch on page 128 shows a simple and satisfactory way. Note the instructions and system adopted for fixing the door, erecting roof and legs.

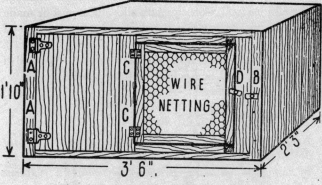

FIG. 27A. BREEDING HUTCH

WIDTH, 2 feet 3 inches.
HEIGHT, 1 foot 10 inches.
LENGTH, 3 feet 6 inches.
One door for total length of hutch, wire netting door hung on the main door.
Other details of construction in chapter on hutches. See special sketch for drainage.
Full length door. Hinged at A, buttons at B.
Small door hinge at C and button at D.
Small wire netting door used for feeding. Full length door for cleaning out.

(See plates of breeding hutches.)

Invariably the inexperienced fix doors with leather hinges, and fastening with bent nails, and doors which are difficult to open or shut. It takes little longer to make a good lasting job, so take the extra trouble.

Badly constructed hutches are not necessary and are time wasted, and prove a constant nuisance and impede proper supervision of stock. Many types of packing cases may be converted into hutches as shown, i.e. tea chests, sugar boxes,

BUCK HUTCH

Stud bucks are matured and need less exercise. Only a small hutch is required; 18 in. square is large enough. It is best to have this hutch away from the breeding does.

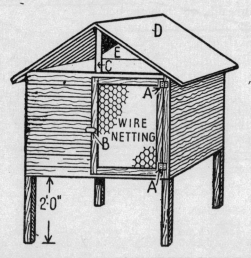

FIG. 28. PACKING CASE CONVERTED INTO HUTCH

Nail 4 uprights at the 4 corners of packing case, 2 inches by 1 inch material. Erect 2 feet from the ground.
A Hinges flat on door and *front* of hutch.
B Button.
C Upright centre front and back, supporting batten for nailing boards for roof D.
D Roof. Plain boards or matching $\frac{1}{2}$ inch by $\frac{5}{8}$ inch. Cover with roofing felt.
E Open space on top of hutch, suitable for storing food in dry.
DOOR, 2 inches by $\frac{3}{4}$ inch framing. $\frac{3}{4}$ inch mesh wire netting nailed on inside of door.
Size according to packing case. Suitable for breeding or buck hutch.

(See chapter on hutches.)

RUNNING-ON HUTCHES

When producing rabbits for meat purposes only, the young are usually weaned and kept together until killed. But when producing for fur and meat, with the intention of producing good skins, they must be grown for a longer period before the skins are in prime condition.

For that purpose, single hutches are necessary after the 4 months stage, otherwise they will fight and badly damage fur and health, especially the bucks.

Small hutches are all that is necessary for this purpose.

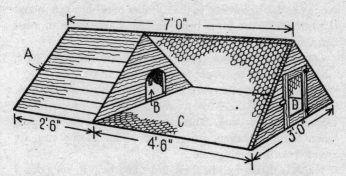

FIG. 32. APEX MORANT HUTCH FOR FOLDING

A Sleeping compartment. Weatherboarded or boarded and felted roof. Plain boards at bottom. Door at end, similar to D.
B Opening for rabbits to enter.
C Wire netting floor 1½ inch mesh. Outside covering of run 1 inch mesh.
D Door at end.
Length 7 feet, width 3 feet. Sleeping compartment 2 feet 6 inches long and run 4 feet 6 inches long.

An economical way is to make 8 hutches in one stack, the size of each compartment to contain one rabbit being 1 ft. 6 in. wide, 2 ft. 3 in. deep and 1 ft. 10 in. high. (*See Plate* 46, *Running-on hutches.*)

For running-on table rabbits up to killing age, small poultry houses with wooden floors are ideal. The approximate size required for an average litter of 6 to 7 is a house 6 ft. long by 2 ft. 6 in. wide.

MORANT HUTCH

A very useful system for growing young stock with the minimum of attention is the type of hutch known as the MORANT. This type is used for folding, the rabbits feeding through the wire netting of the bottom of the run.

This is particularly useful for keeping down the grass on lawns and waste grass in orchards. It is made to move easily, and generally needs moving on to fresh ground at least twice per day according to the number of rabbits put in and the quality of the grass being folded. Large plots of grass can thus be folded off in easy stages.

See the Morant Hutch (Fig. 32). It shows the apex type, which is easy to construct from new materials.

The type more often used is in the form of a coop and run. The bottom of the Morant run should be covered with 1½-inch mesh netting. This prevents the rabbits escaping when folding uneven ground. The sides of the run are covered with 1-inch mesh.

Rabbits thrive well in these units and help to keep down the waste grass. It is important to note feeding is necessary in addition to the folding; grass supplies only part of the necessary diet.

In wet weather it is not advisable to move on to fresh ground so frequently. The same ground should only be folded once each season, and well limed before the next season.

COLONY HUTCH

Breeders who have several litters to wean at the same time, find advantages in a larger type of hutch for running on young stock.

Poultry houses can be used for this purpose also, the usual size being 10 ft. long, 7 ft. wide. Up to 30 rabbits can be weaned in a place of this size.

To keep trace of the records of stock so housed, if required for future breeding purposes, tattoo before allowing them to run together.

CONVERTED POULTRY HOUSE

There are many large poultry houses idle these days, which can very simply and easily be converted into most useful rabbit breeding and rearing units. See plan for converting poultry house design for partitions.

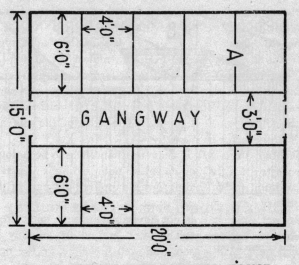

FIG. 33. CONVERTING POULTRY HOUSE

This house is 20 feet by 15 feet and is divided into Running-on pens for Rabbits.
Each pen constructed 6 feet long and 4 feet wide.
Gangway in centre. All doors opening on to gangway.
(*See Fig. 33A on dividing pens in large poultry house.*)

The house can be divided by having a gangway in centre if the house is wide enough, otherwise a gangway at side. Each pen should be 4 ft. wide, 6 ft. or more long, according to the size of the house. Partitions 3 ft. high.

These can be constructed of wood or wire netting, or both.

Feeding is done from over the top, but a door opening out on to the gangway is needed for cleaning out. The usual floor space per head for growing stock is 1½ sq. ft. Young stock grow exceptionally well in these runs, owing to exercise and good ventilation. Some excellent results have been achieved.

These pens can also be used for breeding in, allowing the doe a large sized nest box to have the litter in.

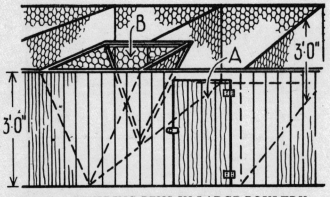

FIG. 33A. DIVIDING PENS IN LARGE POULTRY
HOUSE

Height of all partitions 3 feet.
Width of pens 4 feet.
MATERIALS:—All wood or wood and wire netting ¾ inch to 1 inch mesh.
A Wooden door.
B Hay rack to serve two pens. Construct on wooden framing 2 inch by 1 inch, cover with 1¼ or 1½ inch heavy gauge wire netting.
(See Fig. 33 of conversion of poultry house 20 feet by 15 feet.)

HUTCH FLOORS

A sketch has been given on page 125 of a drainage system for hutch floors. This is specially illustrated because it is of the greatest importance. It is advised to make all hutch floors on this principle when possible. This system keeps the hutch floors clean and dry, and saves a lot of cleaning out.

NEST BOX

Many breeders favour nest boxes for the does to kindle in. These are placed inside the hutch at the darkest corner furthest away from the door.

The advantages are, (*a*) warmth, (*b*) keeps litter dry in damp bottom hutches, (*c*) prevents young from wandering about hutch too soon. The time when nest boxes are of the greatest advantage is during the severe winter weather, from November up to February. Also essential for breeding in open Colony runs. (*See Fig. 34 and specification of nest box.*)

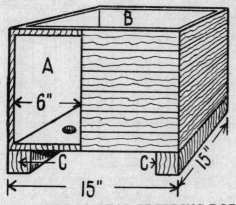

FIG. 34. NEST BOX FOR BREEDING DOES

Made from ordinary box similar to margarine box.
A Opening for mother to enter 6 inches wide.
B Top left open.
C Nail box on 2 inch by 2 inch quartering to keep off bottom of hutch.
Bottom of nest box should have $\frac{3}{4}$ inch holes bored at corners for drainage.

WIRE NETTING FLOORS

Wire netting is often used for hutch floors with the idea of not using litter and improving sanitation. Generally speaking, for table and fur production, stock does not thrive so well as with the boarded floors. Sore hocks frequently develop. Large mesh netting prevents exercise and rabbits are liable to get their feet caught in it. Small mesh netting gets clogged with droppings, making cleaning out operations difficult.

These floors are most suited to Angoras, which need less exercise, and are purely a wool producing rabbit and not described in this book.

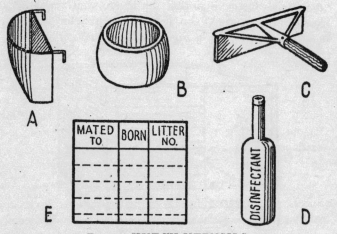

FIG. 35. HUTCH UTENSILS.

A Water feeder. 5 inches by 3 inches by 2¼ inches.
B Feeding Pot. 4½ inches earthenware.
C Cleaning out hoe 6 inch or 9 inch blade.
D Disinfectant.
E Card for breeding record.

LITTER

Bedding litter is used in hutches to soak up any liquid and add to the general comfort of the rabbit. The best kind is wheat straw, next barley and oat straw. Straw, in addition to serving the purpose stated, provides a considerable amount of food of value. Another type of bedding which is good, and generally used by most rabbit breeders, is made by collecting waste grass from the hedgerows and roadside. Bracken, sawdust or peat-moss litter is satisfactory.

CLEANING OUT HUTCHES

How often a hutch should be cleaned out depends on size of hutch and number of rabbits in, and type of litter used. The usual period is once a week. Clear out all litter and droppings. Sprinkle bottom with lime. If any infection in hutch, limewash or creosote. When using the latter allow several days to dry before putting stock in.

UTENSILS

The following are the usual requirements as utensils for the hutch: (1) feeding pot; (2) water drinker; (3) hoe for cleaning out; (4) disinfectant; (5) hutch record card for recording matings, etc. (*See Fig.* 35.)

FEEDING

Success is governed by the initiative of the operator. Although the task that is undertaken is simple, and devoid of outstanding pitfalls, it must from the start be thoroughly understood that rabbits need regular attention, and must be fed during the week-ends and wet days.

A system should be devised at the beginning, allotting certain times of the day for feeding and certain days for cleaning out and other management routine.

Study the habits of the wild rabbit and keep as closely as possible to these ways. The tame rabbit is much the same in every respect. When the tame rabbit escapes, it will thrive beside the wild rabbit, in spite of the plutocratic menu it has been used to in the hutch.

The outstanding points to note with the wild rabbit, and of the greatest importance as a guidance to feeding, is the fact that wild rabbits, although they may be in the midst of abundance of luscious food, will roam further to add to the variety, with the result that they exercise freely between courses and stimulate their digestive organs.

On the other hand the tame rabbit which has not been fed regularly with a varied diet, may suddenly be given an abundance of similar luscious food, and will, without moving, proceed to gorge until its insides have extended to more than double the normal size.

The overtax on its digestive organs results in indigestion and other complications which may prove fatal.

It is not practical to make any hard and fast rule as to the number of meals, quantity and time to feed, but the main rule to bear in mind is to feed a little at a time and often, and to give as big a variation of food as possible.

Make a special study and give as near to the exact amounts that are required as possible. Never overfeed or allow rabbits to get exceedingly hungry. Clear away any food left over from the previous meal.

If stock are found to have gone off their appetite, this may be due to overfeeding. Reduce the rations and gradually return to normal. Master these simple rules and success is assured.

HOURS TO FEED

Arrange the feeding hours to come at regular times, with intervals as far between as possible. Provided the rabbits are clearing up all food given, an additional feed is advantageous.

Continuous feeding may appear to be an obstacle; but as some meals only entail opening the hutch door and putting in a handful of greens, it is not a serious item.

Mated does and youngsters up to 3 months old should be fed 3 times per day: first thing in the morning, midday and last thing at night. Other stock first thing in the morning and last thing at night.

MEALS

It is advisable always to keep to the same rotation in feeding the same types of food. It must be remembered that the first meal in the morning is given when the rabbit is most hungry and liable to gorge.

It is therefore best to give a concentrated food then, or if not feeding a concentrate, use hay. The following scale gives a guidance:

		Morning	Midday	Night
WINTER	{	Mash or Hay	Roots or Scraps	Hay
			Roots or Scraps	Scraps
SUMMER	{	Hay or Mash	Greenfood	Greenfood
			Greenfood	Greenfood

FROZEN FOOD

Frozen roots or greens are injurious to tame rabbits. Stocks of roots and green in winter months should be kept free from frost. If affected, thaw out well before using. Avoid feeding roots after midday in severe winter weather; any not eaten right away will get frozen in the hutch. It is important to give the exact quantity which they will clear in a reasonable time. Otherwise clear out at night any left over.

FERMENTED FOOD

It is very important when feeding fresh greens such as clover and grass not to allow fermentation. After gathering lay out thinly in open shed. Silage is not suitable for rabbits. It can be made so, and experiments are being conducted.

WET GREENS

There is much difference of opinion as to whether greens should be fed wet or dry. Generally speaking, dry greens are best. If wet greens are used, the change should be brought about gradually. Wet greens are more liable to cause scours. Observation should be kept.

FRESH GREENS

It depends on the type of greens and time of the year as to whether greens should be wilted before using. If the greens are young and succulent, it is advisable to wilt in the sun for a few hours. When grass or clovers are more matured and lose much of their sap, it is not beneficial to wilt. When greens have been lying close to the ground in a wet period and become yellow, dry off thoroughly and wilt before using.

MASH

There are two ways of using mash, one in the dry form, and the other to mix the mash with water into a dry, crumbly form.

COOKED FOODS

Potatoes are the only food which need cooking before feeding. All other roots and greens are best fed raw. In order to ease the meal rations, it is advantageous to boil roots, and dry off with weatings and/or bran. Sugar beet is particularly useful for this purpose.

KITCHEN UTENSIL

Every household should have 2 good-sized pails in a corner of the kitchen to collect all household scraps; one for green waste, the other for potatoes and peelings, used for mash.

(*See section dealing with household scraps.*) Those who have no rabbits should pass their scraps on to others.

FOODS

Rabbits are most accommodating in their habits of feeding, in as much as they will eat almost anything, and generally speaking they will eat that which comes most readily to hand.

As the object of this book is to explain how householders can produce rabbit meat from scraps, it is the primary object to explain how rabbits can be kept without relying on imported foodstuffs and the purchasing of foods from farmers.

The word 'scraps' is used rather for the want of a more descriptive word. A new word to cover this title certainly needs coining.

Waste rather implies that the householder is neglectful. Swill gives the impression of a smelly container with hoards of flies. In this case waste or scraps is meant to imply food suitable for rabbits which would otherwise go to waste, this arising from vegetable garden, kitchen and hedgerow.

Each of these yield an abundance of rabbit food and only need a small amount of trouble and inconvenience in the leisure hours to be brought to most valuable use of the utmost national importance. The foods required are mostly surplus to existing requirements.

A system must be devised in order to collect more than sufficient food for the immediate needs. Store up sufficient or the winter months when food is most plentiful. Winter seasons are more difficult to cater for.

To eliminate the worry of a shortage in certain winter months, it is advisable to use up any waste ground or part of the garden to produce stocks for the difficult feeding period.

ROTATION OF GREENFOOD AND ROOTS, FOR EACH MONTH OF THE YEAR. FROM GARDEN AND HEDGEROW. CHIEFLY WASTE.

Month	Varieties of Food	Observations
January	Swedes, Sugar Beet, Carrots, Cabbage	Mainly Roots
February	Swedes, Sugar Beet, Carrots, Cabbage, Kale	Mainly Roots
March	Sugar Beet, Carrots, Brussels Sprout Tops and Stalks. Shoots from other garden greens. Thousand-headed Kale	Greens beginning to be good
April	Brussels Sprout Tops and Stalks, Cabbage leaves, Thousand-headed Kale, Hedge Parsley, Young Grass, Dandelions, Chickweed. Finish up any Sugar Beet and Carrots, Gap Kale	Abundance of wild plants and waste
May	Use any remaining greens in garden if not on flower. Hedge Parsley, Dandelions, Plantain, Grass, Spring Cabbage, Waste, Lawn Mowings, Gap Kale	Super-abundance of wasted Greenfood, Garden and Hedgerow
June	Dandelions, Plantain, Grass, Lawn Mowings, Spring Cabbage, Waste, thinnings from Carrots and other Greens, Chicory, Gap Kale	Abundance of food. Grass very good this month

July	Grass, Lawn Mowings (if not dried up), Carrot and Green thinnings, Pea Pods and Haulm, Perpetual Kale Shoots, Chicory, Coltsfoot, Mallow, Groundsel	Grasses getting dried, feed young plants, i.e. thinnings
August	Grass, Lawn Mowings (if not dried up), Carrot and Green thinnings, Pea Pod and Haulm, Kale Plants, Perpetual Kale, Chicory, Groundsell, Mallow, Hogweed	Good succulent green getting scarce
September	Second cut Grasses, Lawn Mowings (if green), Carrots and Tops, outside leaves of Brussels Sprouts, Cabbage thinnings, Hogweed, Groundsell, Chicory and Kales	Gradual change to roots. Feed sparingly
October	Carrots, Cabbage, Brussels Sprout leaves, Chicory, Parsnips, Perpetual Kale, Thousand-headed Kale	Chiefly roots. Give variety
November	Kohl Rabi, Marrowstem Kale, Carrots, Sugar Beet	Chiefly roots. Getting matured
December	Kohl Rabi, Marrowstem Kale, Carrots, Sugar Beet, Cabbages	Chiefly roots. Don't feed frosted

From April to the end of September, suitable green-foods are most plentiful, and the scraps and surplus will supply the needs. The recommended lay-out for the garden is dealt with in a separate chapter.

It is not proposed to describe feeding methods which have in the past been used successfully when all types of food-stuffs were plentiful and cheap, and labour-saving devices of the utmost importance. For this purpose labour is considered of minor importance, and classed under the heading of 'scraps or surplus', and considered as time which would otherwise be wasted.

We have emphasised at all stages of this book the importance of giving a large variety of foods. This tends to make feeding easier, giving a large scope to the operator. It is advisable to disillusion the unthinking section of the community who consider tea leaves and lettuce, or cabbage and bran, constitute the entire menu for a rabbit.

HOUSEHOLD SCRAPS

All waste or surplus from vegetables is good food, also any 'left-overs' from breakfast, dinner, tea and supper table. Tea leaves, coffee grounds, bones, kipper skins and other fish waste, fat, rinds of cheese, bread, porridge, apple peels, cooked potatoes and the peelings.

In fact there is no known waste from human edible food which is harmful in moderation.

Devise a system for collecting all this waste.

All kitchen scraps can be used as a basis for the mash. Remember to use fresh. Decayed or putrid food is unsuitable.

Put aside two containers in the kitchen, one for vegetable waste and the other for meat and fish waste, and make sure that every piece of waste is saved. Do not be content with using your own scraps; get others to save for you. There are plenty of people too busily occupied, or maybe some too lazy and unpatriotic to exert themselves and undertake any work of national importance.

GARDEN SURPLUS

All vegetable gardens yield a vast amount of surplus and waste which is the ideal food for rabbits. Practically all vegetables have surplus parts which are not used in the kitchen. The outside leaves and stalks of all cabbage varieties give an abundance of good feeding.

Turnip tops, carrot tops and thinnings, parsnips, celery tops, pea haulm, pea pods, beetroot, artichokes, apples and shoots from fruit trees, are among the principal and most useful.

Don't use potato tops, broad bean haulm, rhubarb.

Lettuce should be used only in moderation.

The flower garden yields good foods, but these are few and far between, and many are poisonous, especially the seeds and pods. It is advisable to refrain from using any flower unless you have a definite knowledge as to which are suited and those that are not. Otherwise confine the menu from the flower garden to weeds.

CULTIVATED GREENFOODS

The sketch and chapter dealing with the growing of rabbit foods gives the details for growing greens and roots to safeguard the period when food is at its shortest.

In addition to those advocated for growing in spare garden ground, there are other very excellent greenfoods which are grown chiefly on farms, but some where there is a plentiful supply growing wild. These varieties chiefly interest the commercial breeder who cannot spare the labour for the gathering of the wild plants.

The most important of these varieties are Red Clover, White Clover, Sainfoin, Trefoil, Tares and Lucerne. Those referred to, with the exception of Lucerne, are annuals. There is the permanent White Clover, but on most soils it cannot be depended on to give a regular annual yield.

Lucerne is a valuable green, and is usually put down in a 7 years' lay; during that period it can be cut on an average of four times a year and is a very heavy cropper. It takes two seasons to establish.

WILD GREENFOOD

A most important matter is to become acquainted with the best varieties of wild greenfood and to avoid using any plants which are injurious.

It is difficult to describe these in a way which can be understood by all.

It is therefore advisable if possible to gain this knowledge from some local rabbit keeper.

Wild plants are known by many names in different parts of the country. Often the correct name is unknown. The following are the most valuable and commonly used: clovers, vetches, coltsfoot, chickweed, docks (leaves only), dandelions, groundsel, knotgrass, comfrey, hogweed, mallow, plantains, shepherd's purse, sow-thistle, hedge parsley and practically all grasses, excepting the coarse types and those growing on swampy ground. Use vetches and other wild plants before they seed. Some pods and seeds, especially vetches, contain a mild poison.

LEAVES AND SHOOTS

Most leaves and young shoots of trees are a good food. Oak, hazel, and elm are the best. Quantities of these can be gathered at ease, and help to supplement the garden waste when short. It is advantageous to give pieces of wood with bark on. This supplies valuable nourishment and prevents gnawing of hutches.

LAWN MOWINGS

Lawn mowings can be used with excellent results, but must be used fresh or properly dried. They must NOT be allowed to heat (ferment). If stored before using, lay out 1 in. thick on a sack. Avoid using if covered with dust or dirt. The type of lawn which has a good herbage containing white clover is the best.

Buttercups and daisies are not good.

Avoid putting mowings in heaps. It is possible to dry in sun by laying out thinly and storing for winter months. This can only be done in dry, hot weather. They then form an excellent and valuable food which can also be used in mash if required.

ACORNS

Lack of organisation and interest in this country is the cause of thousands of tons of acorns, a most valuable concentrated food, going to waste. If properly dried they can be used throughout the winter. Persevere and collect all possible, when your concentrated food problem will be overcome.

A small handful is sufficient for one adult rabbit. Gather the acorns as soon as they fall, lay out thinly to dry for a considerable time. An open shed is the best for this purpose. Make sure they are absolutely dry before storing for the winter. Don't feed if they have been heated or mouldy. Must be perfectly dry.

HAY

It is of the utmost importance to have a store of hay for the winter months. Sufficient for the ordinary size rabbitry can easily be collected from waste ground, orchards and hedgerows. An open shed is the best means for storing, it keeps the hay dry while collecting and using.

Don't leave the hay in the sun to bake up. Small heaps of

hay can be collected quite green. A small amount of heating
is advisable, it improves the quality and sweetens the hay.
When purchasing hay, get the best clover or grass hay with
a good herbage. AVOID BUYING OVER-HEATED HAY,
THE TYPE WITH THE GREEN LEAF ON IS THE BEST.
Rank grasses make poor hay for rabbits and are chiefly
suitable for litter. Never feed mouldy or damp.

NETTLES

Nettles are a good food for rabbits, but should not be fed
freshly cut. Cut and lay out to dry at least 12 hours before
feeding. They make good hay, if stored when green. Cut
before they get old and coarse. There is little feeding value
when old and going to seed, and they are not appetising at
that stage.

POTATOES

One of the most valuable feeding stuffs for rabbits is the
potato, and it can tide breeders over many difficulties in
feeding.

Potatoes are suitable for all ages and for does in milk.
They can be fed in many ways and give excellent results.

The easiest and most common way to use, is to boil, dry
off, then mix into a crumbly mash with meal.

When meal is exceptionally short, boil the potatoes in a
small amount of water. Allow most of the water to boil
away and leave the potatoes almost dry, they will consequently absorb less meal when making into mash, and can
in fact be cooked in this way to a dry state suitable for use
without mash.

It is practical to bake for storing and feed without mash.
This can be done extensively when people have coal ovens.
Using the oven when ever available.

Cut into slices, and lay in flat pans in the oven until
absolutely dry.

This takes several hours. Store away in tins if possible.

Small potatoes which are commonly known as 'chats' are suitable and most generally used. Anyone unable to get supplies should apply to the Ministry of Agriculture who undertake to put breeders in touch with suppliers of special animal feeding potatoes.

ROOTS

To take the place of greenfood in the winter months, it is helpful to have supplies of ROOTS.

Carrots, parsnips and sugar beet can be used throughout the autumn and winter months up to April. Kohl Rabi can be used when ready up to Christmas. Swedes from November up to the middle of February. Mangolds from Christmas up to the summer or as long as they keep sound. It is not advisable to use any of these roots before the stated time.

SUGAR BEET

A special paragraph is deemed necessary to stress the importance of sugar beet for rabbits.

This valuable root in an average season contains 17 per cent sugar in addition all the other constituents of mangolds and swedes, and is therefore a self-contained bulk and concentrate.

It can be fed in slices as roots, making mash unnecessary, or boiled with the potatoes mashing the potatoes and sugar beet together, using the pulp and liquid for mash. It is necessary to obtain a licence for growing sugar beet for household use, but is NOT necessary if grown for feeding purposes.

CORN

The best corn for rabbits is oats, squashed for preference. Barley and wheat is good in moderation. Corn is best used in the offal forms, being most digestible and less wasteful.

MASH

The definition which applies to meal as used for rabbits, is a mixture of offals milled from cereals.

These can be used in wet or dry form. Wet mash really means damped and given in a crumbly state, not too sticky. Dry mash is wasteful and not so appetising.

The amount to be given to an adult rabbit is usually a small handful the size of a tangerine. Amount, however, varying according to ingredients, also age and size of rabbit.

In the days of plenty an excellent mash consisted of soaking flaked maize in the amount of water it would absorb, and drying off into a crumbly state with bran and weatings, all equal parts in weight, adding half a part Sussex ground oats, or even better, to use potatoes instead of flaked maize.

Never use mash when stale; it goes sour in a few hours, and is injurious to all stock.

Clear out of hutch any mash left over from previous meal. Mash should now be made principally from potatoes and house scraps, dried off with bran and/or weatings. This constitutes a really sound mash on which breeders can expect the best results.

WATER

Generally speaking, water is necessary for rabbits, especially for does when kindling, also when greenfood is lacking in moisture, particularly in the hot weather. When feeding roots in the winter, especially mangolds and swedes which contain a large percentage of water, it is not necessary.

Give fresh each day and keep containers clean.

GROWING RABBIT FOOD IN THE GARDEN

In addition to the large amount of rabbit food which arises

in the garden, it is a great advantage to make provision for winter feeding, especially for those who intend having a good size rabbitry.

Although supplies can be got from market gardeners and farmers, your national war effort will be of more importance if the undertaking is made self-supporting, and the total output a personal affair. Most people have some spare ground in the garden under cultivation, or are able to

GAP KALE	CHICORY
CATTLE CARROTS	MARROW STEM KALE
SWEDES	KOHL RABI
	PERPETUAL KALE
SUGAR BEET	THOUSAND HEADED KALE

VARIETIES OF FOODS TO CULTIVATE
Plan gives lay-out in proportions of each variety required.

acquire some. Failing this there is usually waste ground such as orchards or other plots, crying for cultivation.

It is surprising what a bulk of food can be raised from a small plot of ground, and how useful an odd corner of the garden can be if put down to chicory or a few cattle carrots.

For the cultivation of all rabbit foods, it is of the greatest advantage to add a good dressing of rotted rabbit manure.

If the ground has not been recently manured put on one good sized barrow load to 10 square yards, and if possible cover 9 in. deep. This will enable the crop to withstand drought, excessive wet and frost.

If litter is used which may be considered injurious to the soil, burn heaps on the ground intended for cultivation. It is not proposed to go into details on cultivations; the fullest information will be found in *The Penguin Book of Food Growing, Storing and Cooking*, written by F. W. P. Carter.

The chart on Varieties of Foods to Cultivate gives a suggested lay-out of foods for feeding during the short period. This is drawn to scale, showing the proportions of each to grow. It is not practical to give dimensions as so much depends on the available ground and number of stock kept.

A plot of ground 20 ft. square, if in good cultivation, can yield sufficient food to tide the small breeder over the winter period, and make rabbit keeping a very easy matter.

For cases when unable or not prepared to cultivate for the purpose, but anxious to fill in gaps in the garden, thousand-headed kale should be used, and for the odd pieces of ground, grow sugar beet and chicory. The intention of this book is to assist the breeder operating on a moderate scale, and the accompanying chart is compiled with the assumption that an abundance of food is available and going to waste in the spring and summer months, and there is no need to cater for that period in the garden or allotment. It is only the large commercial rabbit breeder who has to make provision for that period. A few hours with the spade will be well rewarded.

KILLING, SKINNING AND PREPARING CARCASE

Having successfully reared some rabbits for table, the

CULTIVATED FOODS

Variety	Period to Sow	When to Feed	How to Use	Merits	Cultivation
Gap Kale	May to August	April to May	Feed fresh	Useful when other Kale are exhausted	Sow thinly where required
Cattle Carrots ..	Early March to July	From September to March	Fresh or clamp for later use. Use tops fresh	Thinning very useful. Good digestive food	Sow where required. Thin out 20 inches apart
Swedes	March to middle of July	November to March	Clamp in October	Excellent root in winter	Sow where required. Chop out and single 6 to 9 inches apart
Sugar Beet	March to June	October to April	Clamped before use or fresh out of ground	Most valuable. Contain up to 18% sugar and root value	Sow where required. Chop out and single to 5 inches apart × 18 inches
Chicory	March to June	Summer months	Fresh	Good yield, constant picking	Sow in rows where required. Don't single out
Marrowstem Kale ..	March to June	September to April Best before Christmas	Fresh. Divide Stems	Contains root and green value	Thin out 12 inches × 2 feet or transplant
Kohl Rabi	February to	October to Christmas	Fresh	Very nutritious and safe root	Sow in seed bed, transplant when 3 inches apart
Perpetual Kale ..	March to September	March to November	Fresh	Useful in case of green shortage summer	From cuttings only. Plant 18 inches each way
Thousandheaded Kale	February to June	July to May	Fresh	Heavy yielder. A very good food	Sow where required or in seed beds. Transplant when 3 inches high or chop out 15 inches each way

question arises as to how to get the skinning and carcase prepared to the best advantage.

This is an easy operation and although it may take quite a time with the first few, little skill is necessary and speed will follow.

It takes an experienced skinner 30 seconds to take the skin off an average rabbit. Photographs show the various stages of this operation. If these photographs are studied and the following instructions observed, beginners should not experience the slightest difficulty.

It is important for all breeders to persevere and do their own killing, skinning and preparing of the carcase, unless local services can be acquired and prepared to operate on the lines shown. All rabbit skins have value, and it is important that no matter what type, the skin should be handled carefully. Any quantity are needed for export, and the production of these skins can play a big part in bringing in dollars.

KILLING AGE FOR MEAT

Four months old upwards is the usual killing age for table rabbits, and provided they are well grown, they make excellent carcases at this age. If feeding stuffs are particularly plentiful, grow on for a longer period. Carcases are really prime up to 10 months old.

KILLING FOR PELT

If the best prime skins are required, the age for pelting is *from 6 months upwards*, depending on the time of the year and season. Best skins are obtained round Christmas.

The pelting season for prime skins is from October up to April. If pelted when not in prime condition the pelt is of much less value. It is advisable at times to kill off stock regardless of skin value, when it is considered it will take the rabbit a long time to moult out.

Fur rabbits are also used in the same way as table rabbits and killed at all stages for the carcase trade.

To determine whether a rabbit is ready to pelt needs great care, and only experience will give the best results.

First note the general appearance of the fur. Make sure that it is sleek and shows no obvious signs of moult.

Then examine more closely, blow the fur back, and look for young hair shooting up from base.

If patches of young hair are found, usually in circles, this proves the rabbit is still moulting or in some cases is due to fighting. If the latter it may be advantageous to pelt, as the other part of the skin may be prime and start moulting before the other patches clear.

The skin should be clear white if the rabbit is in prime coat. Usually rabbits are in prime coat for a very short time. In cold periods round Christmas they remain in coat for quite a time.

Do not pelt before you are sure the rabbit is ready; better late than early. Any black patches on the skin side of the pelt when dried denote moult. This serves as a guidance when selecting other stock, to the inexperienced.

Rabbits usually finish their moult at (a) *neck*, (b) *flanks and rump*, (c) *centre back*. There is no definite rule as they vary with seasons, but it is characteristic that in seasons all rabbits finish their moult in a certain place.

The prime skin is the product of a fully matured rabbit, and is in the biggest demand at the highest prices. These are usually the chief aim of commercial rabbit breeders.

There are, however, other stages when the fur is in full coat. At 4 to 5 months, rabbits will be found to come into full coat for a short time, and skins have a considerable value. For those intending to breed fur rabbits with meat as the primary object, this is an important side to the

business. With this object in view, meat is the product and
skins the by-product, and the latter can come to the most
money. It is important to note that at 4 to 5 months killing
stage, the rabbits will come into this intermediate coat at
different stages.

Some rabbits mature quicker than others; with slow
growing rabbits the skin development is retarded. A very
small percentage never come in at this stage at all. This
system should receive every attention for present-day needs.

The earliest stage at which rabbits can be pelted is 6 weeks
old, when they come into full baby coat. From 1920 onwards
for a number of years, breeders were producing large
quantities of these baby Chinchilla skins and getting from
3/- to 6/- each for them. These skins were used for the
trimming trade, to imitate the real chinchilla.

KILLING

The best method to kill is by the dislocation of the neck, the
same as with poultry (*see plate* 48). Take the rabbit by the
hind legs in the right hand, and the back of the head with
the left, stretch out straight, force the head back, and at
the same time with a quick jerk of the left hand dislocate
the neck. Remember to keep the rabbit fully stretched at
the same time as jerking the head back and pulling. Death
is instantaneous. After this operation, hang up on a string
suspended from a beam, passing the leg through a loop in
the string at hock.

Hang for 5 minutes before proceeding to skin. This allows
the blood to drain to the head, rendering the flesh white. If
skinned immediately after killing, the flesh will be red, and
skinning made difficult with blood.

PELTING

In the fur trade, generally speaking, pelt means raw skin,

and skin the pelt after dressing. The operation of taking the skin off, is known as pelting. This is started by suspending the rabbit by its hind leg from a string at a convenient height for working. (*See Plate* 49.)

A sharp-pointed knife is required. Insert knife at hock and cut down to the vent on the inside of the leg. There is usually a natural joining of fur indicating this position. Then cut up from vent, to the hock of other leg. Pull out the tail part on the skin. Slip the skin right down over the forelegs with left hand; at the same time cut any thin skin impeding progress.

If possible allow all fat to remain on carcase.

Great care should be taken not to cut any of the pelt, and not at this stage to sever the insides.

Clear the front legs, severing at hocks, slip over neck clearing up to ears, cut off at base of ears, and by careful pulling and manipulation with the knife, the skin should come whole off the rabbit. This method is termed *skinning in the sleeve fashion*.

DIVIDING PELT

Having taken the pelt off, proceed to cut down from the vent, down the centre of the belly to the mouth. Knife needs to be very sharp.

Hold pelt with the left hand, operating the knife slowly, saw fashion. There is a natural seam on the skin side of the pelt, which should be followed. (*See Plate* 50.)

DRESSING CARCASE

Dressed tame rabbits are known by most consumers as Ostend rabbits. Ostend was the biggest collecting centre for packing dressed rabbits for the London market.

In order to obtain the best prices, these carcases were all dressed and packed in a uniform fashion.

The style about to be described is the best and is known as the Ostend fashion. Carcases should be handled in this way for all purposes. (*See Plates* 54–8.)

After pelting unstring the carcase. Insert knife at hock, between sinew and leg. Cut a hole large enough to thread the other leg through, threading in the hole at the back side of the leg, then force both legs back to the rear as far as possible. Open up at pelvis joint, and again force the legs back, making a parting at the joint $\frac{3}{4}$ in. wide.

Remove the gut and any excreta. This is of the utmost importance.

If any of the excreta is allowed to remain, flesh in this immediate vicinity will become tainted. Hang the carcase on a nail driven in a beam and proceed to remove the insides.

Insert first two fingers of the left hand in hole already made, pull the skin away from the inside, and guide the knife down the centre of belly between these two fingers. Cut only the outside skin, avoiding any of the insides; cut down to within 2 in. from where the ribs commence. This operation is shown clearly by the plates.

Then with the left hand remove all insides excepting kidney, fat and liver, severing at the part where the paunch joins the liver.

The liver should then be replaced in the carcase.

If the skin has been cut down too low, it will be difficult to replace the liver and the carcase must be left to hang.

This operation is simple. All the entrails not required come out in one handful. Avoid breaking any of the gut, and keep the carcase as clean as possible.

Unless an accident has happened during the operation, such as breaking the paunch, which makes the carcase dirty, never use water on the carcase.

The hanging drains all blood away, and the carcase should be perfectly dry and clean when set. Then cut off front paws at joints, and make small insertions one each side of the ribs, in which tuck the front legs. (*See Plate* 58.)

The hind feet should then be chopped off, leaving only $1\frac{1}{2}$ in. with fur on, next to where the legs are threaded.

MARKETING CARCASE

Having completed the operation of dressing the carcase, allow to hang until completely cold and set. If possible, it is best to kill in the evening and allow the carcase to hang all night, ready for packing the next morning.

Twelve hours is the minimum time to hang before packing. If packing for transport, line hamper or box with greaseproof paper. Newspaper is not suitable, the print coming off on to the carcase. They travel better wrapped in bulk this way, than to wrap up each carcase separately in paper. At the time of publication the maximum retail price is controlled at 1/7 per lb.

Special reference at the beginning of this book is made regarding controlling of prices and coupons for rationing.

NAILING PELTS

Having cut the skin down (as described on page 155 – Dividing Skins) the next step is to nail the skin on a board for drying.

For this purpose, drying boards are made by nailing $\frac{1}{2}$-inch boards together with splines to measure 30 in. long and 18 in. wide. A door or side of box is satisfactory.

Then place the wet skin flat on the drying board, fur down, and proceed to nail out. Start by putting a nail at each corner, bottom part of the skin first. The head part should be on board furthest from you.

Judgment has to be used as to the exact position of the first 4 nails. The skin has to be stretched moderately, and stretched up to the position of the nails already in, leaving the sides of the skin as even as possible, using as many nails as are needed, to get the desired effect.

Nails should be driven as near to the edge of the skin as possible. The average stretched size of a skin from an adult rabbit of medium to large size variety of rabbit, is 17 in. long and 14 in. wide. For drying the best quality skins, this system is preferable to using stretchers.

STRETCHING PELTS

A simple method for drying skins, and a way in which all the Australian wild skins are handled, is to pull the skin on a stretcher as soon as taken off the rabbit.

For this system, the skin should not be cut down the centre.

There are two main types of stretchers, wire or wood.

They vary in size according to the type of rabbit for which they are required, and for ordinary purposes 3 sizes are used, and size used for adult rabbits measures 7 in. wide at top, tapering to 3 in. wide at neck, and 18 in. long.

Having placed the stretcher inside the skin, the top part where the opening is, is pulled up to the top and hooked on the wire stretcher and nailed on the wood stretcher.

DRYING

As soon as the skin is nailed or put on a stretcher, proceed to dry. This operation should not be delayed for more than a day or so in damp weather.

The usual time taken to dry a skin is 3 to 4 days. Seven days to 10 days is all right, but never dry under 2 days; to hasten the operation and use excessive heat will render the skin useless. Place the skin in a warm, dry place. The kitchen or boiler room is most suitable. Air in addition to heat is necessary, so airing cupboards should be avoided.

Skins can be dried satisfactorily outside in the spring and

summer. Avoid putting in direct sun. In the winter months, especially November and December, artificial drying is necessary. Never put directly in front of a fire.

FATTING PELTS

When pelts are partly dry, and the fat set, remove all surplus skin and fat by scraping with a blunt knife.

Only remove any surplus which is obviously such. On no account disturb the natural skin of the pelt, then complete the drying. Failing to remove fat from the pelt causes an organic reaction, rendering that part of the skin useless for furriers' purposes, and seriously affecting the value.

STORING PELTS

When pelts are absolutely dry, take off the boards and stretchers, and NOT before. On any suspicion of the skin side of the pelt not being thoroughly dried through, give the benefit of the doubt and dry further.

Skins not thoroughly dried will damp off in damp weather and start decomposing and ferment. Store by packing fur to fur, and skin to skin.

Raw pelts at this stage are susceptible to attacks by various insects and weevils, which breed and multiply rapidly and soon destroy the pelt. This can be avoided by examining frequently, and shaking before re-making the bundles.

If intended to store for any considerable period, dust each skin thoroughly with flaked naphthalene (specially prepared for furriers). If correctly dried, they can be stored in a dry place of even temperature, for any length of time.

MARKETING PELTS

Skins are in the best demand raw.

Furriers prefer to have the skins dressed by their own dressers, and for export there is in most countries a prohibitive tax for the entry for any skins which have been dressed or treated.

There are many reliable firms anxious to buy any quantity of rabbit skins, and most advertise in the fur trade papers. It is advisable to market in minimum quantities of 12 or 20.

Small breeders should co-operate and market in lots of 100 upwards and get the best prices.

When sending small numbers by parcel post, place fur to fur and roll in a bundle. Creasing causes permanent damage. If in any doubts regarding the firm you are sending to, insist on having an offer made for them, subject to your acceptance, you agreeing to refund postage if the price is not acceptable.

DRESSING SKINS

The curing of skins, rendering them suitable and lasting for manufacture, is, in the fur trade, termed dressing. Dressing is essentially a highly skilled trade.

It is not advisable to undertake this work at home, and certainly not without expert advice. It can be done with success, but more often than not a complete failure renders the skin useless.

It is best to get the dressing done by those who specialise in the work, and have the suitable machinery. Addresses of a number of these firms can be found in the advertisement columns of *The British Fur Trade Journal.*

The process of dressing is, to soak in water, then flesh over a special fleshing knife or machine, taking off surplus skin, reducing the thickness and rendering supple, then soaking in pickle, later drying in sawdust and cleaning in a drum, and finally stretching, setting and drying.

MANUFACTURING

Making the dressed skins into a finished article is a highly skilled trade. For coats, capes, collars, etc., special patterns are used. Those intending to have articles made from their skins are best advised to have the work done by an experienced manufacturing furrier.

The following gives a general idea of the work entailed:

Before cutting, the skins are damped, stretched and nailed out and dried, then joined together with a fur-stitching machine, and again damped and stretched to a size slightly larger than the required pattern. Skins joined together in this fashion are known as plates.

The pattern is then placed on the plate and marked, then cut out, by cutting the skin side with a sharp furrier's knife. Then taped at edges, interlining added and finally silk lined.

GROW YOUR FUR COAT

It is the ambition of many to grow sufficient rabbits to produce skins for a fur coat. Before starting this undertaking, it must be remembered that it is necessary to have a good selection to choose from to get a matched coat bundle of skins.

A full length coat takes just over 40 average skins, a three-quarter coat 34, and short coats 22, allowing for average size skins from tame rabbits.

Skins must match in colour, length and density to give the correct appearance. *It is necessary to produce more than double the required number to make a suitable selection.*

The ambitions of smaller breeders should be limited to producing sufficient skins for an attractive cape, which would only use from 5 to 10 skins. Gloves and moccasins are also very attractive and useful articles made from rabbit skins.

HATTERS' FURRIERS

When tame rabbit skins are not up to quality for the manufacturing furrier, they are used by the hatters' furriers.

Hatters' furriers specialise in taking the fur off the skin, and treating it. This product known as furfelt is principally used for making hats. Skins damaged by moult and not fully furred are marketed for this purpose. Wild rabbit skins are the chief source of supply to this trade.

To obtain best prices for wild rabbit skins they should be handled in the same way as described under Nailing Pelts – also Stretching Pelts.

FREQUENT QUESTIONS AND THEIR ANSWERS

Q. *Cannot get my doe mated, have tried frequently.*

A. Try again. Do you put in buck's hutch? If not, you should. Is she too fat or too thin? Is she already mated? Are you sure she is a doe? Read paragraph on mating; also sexing.

Q. *Doe eats her young. Is it because I handled the babies?*

A. Definitely no. Rabbits do not as a rule eat their young because they are handled. Usually it is not her fault, but yours. Does generally eat their young through one of the following causes: Difficulty in kindling, and suffering severe pain. No milk for the babies. Thirsty at time of kindling and no water. Worried by rats, cats or dogs.

Q. *All my youngsters keep dying at 5 weeks old. Why?*

A. Generally because the doe has reared them badly and they lost their baby fat at too early a stage, caused through the mother giving insufficient milk, possibly owing to wrong feeding and insufficient milk-forming food. Read chapters relating to this.

Q. *I bought a rabbit and it died within 7 days. All my stock are strong and healthy, and this rabbit was fed in the same way. Should I expect my money back?*

A. Definitely no. If the rabbit arrived in good condition, the cause was undoubtedly through your management. Change of food. Too much dry food or young greenfood.

Fresh stock should have careful feeding. First feed in moderation, with a good variety of food and not too much of any particular kind.

Q. *I feed my rabbits exactly as described in this book and they still die.*

A. Maybe your stock was in bad stamina when you studied rules on feeding and management laid down in this book, or possibly you are not suited to managing live stock. Read all instructions again and have another try. If you have average intelligence you should be successful.

Q. *I cannot get my bran rations, what shall I do?*

A. Unless you have a lot of rabbits don't worry. Save all household scraps and get your neighbours also. Bran is not altogether essential, but in any case the Domestic Poultry Keepers' Council is there to help you.

Q. *Now I have produced rabbits ready to kill, and have not the heart to kill them. Unless you can recommend a way out shall have to give them up.*

A. Apply to the secretary of your local Rabbit Committee. Failing this ask your local butcher or poulterer to help you out. There are also buyers who specialise in buying alive for the meat trade.

Q. *I sent some young rabbits for a post-mortem examination. The report came back to the effect that they had coccidiosis, acute inflammation of the bowels, with the intestines badly infected, and the statement that it was highly contagious.*

A. The report is undoubtedly correct; read paragraph on coccidiosis. It is often considered the breeder's fault. Affected stock of the same age may not live. Study feeding and management more carefully, and no further trouble should be experienced.

Q. *A breeder tells me he never gives water and has the best results.*

A. It is clearly advised to give water in this book. Yet rabbits can be managed without with excellent results. It is not intended to describe all methods, only those which are considered best.

Q. *My rabbit has suddenly become bad-tempered and attempts to savage me.*

A. This is generally caused by rough handling or frightened by rats or dogs. Sometimes it develops naturally.

Q. *Can I feed on grass, cabbages and roots only?*

A. In the summer, yes, but in winter months difficult. With plenty of good hay, good results are obtained.

DISEASES

With rabbits there is no serious infectious disease. Many would-be beginners have been put off the project through wrong advice of others who have stated that all their rabbits suddenly died off from 'some unknown disease'!

Invariably people who have lost their rabbits in this way, should blame themselves entirely.

The usual cause of numerous deaths in the rabbitry is through neglect or bad food.

It is not the object of this book to pass over any difficulties, and it can be assumed that any complaints are of unimportant character, and if dealt with promptly need cause no further anxiety.

When noticing the slightest trouble with any rabbit, isolate at once – then doctor it; if it does not yield to the cure, destroy. Adopt a method in the rabbitry so that hutches and feeding utensils are cleaned at regular intervals.

Disease can be spread rapidly by not putting the same feeding dish back to the same rabbit each time. The following are the most frequent complaints.

COCCIDIOSIS

Rabbits contract a similar kind of coccidiosis as poultry.

This complaint is more prevalent in wet weather, especially when feeding with green which has been lying close to the ground, and consequently affected with the coccidia.

Symptoms. Young rabbits suddenly die off without any apparent reason, lose the use of their legs, and fade away. Seemingly strong youngsters lose their condition in a few days, retaining their appetite right up to the last. Youngsters from 6 to 12 weeks are the usual sufferers. If opened the intestines will be found to be punctured in many places. The general effect is, that it makes the rearing of youngsters difficult for a period.

On the other hand if stock is strong and healthy, they are usually able to resist attacks without ill effects. Do not be pessimistic on receiving a post-mortem report stating your rabbit died from coccidiosis. In certain seasons a big percentage of rabbits, without the breeder's knowledge, have this complaint, and if they die maybe from some other primary cause, it is invariably attributed to coccidiosis.

The remedy should be chiefly in the form of improving the condition of your stock. Usually the complaint is aggravated by greenfood, therefore change the diet GRADUALLY. Also, if the greenfood can be cut a few inches from the ground, and not allowed to touch the soil, it may overcome the trouble.

Some mothers can be carriers. If suspected, put on wire netting floors, preventing the droppings coming in contact with the food. Feed all greens and hay in hayracks, preventing the greens coming in contact with the droppings.

Another remedy is to feed entirely on dry food and water, consisting of good hay and mash, until the trouble ceases. The usual procedure adopted by experienced breeders is to increase the amount of dry food, chiefly hay.

Endeavour to improve the condition by more frequent feeding, and the trouble will soon cease.

It is considered important to give the foregoing explanation, although the actual seriousness of the trouble really does not justify it.

But because scientists give so much prominence to the disease and usually over-stress the seriousness and often give such alarming reports that breeders are convinced they will never be able to make a success of rabbit breeding.

Many, including the author, are of the opinion that all human beings have consumption germs at some period, but they are kept under unless they have a serious breakdown in health, when the disease will flourish beyond control, and the same applies to coccidiosis with rabbits.

SNUFFLES

When rabbits develop fits of sneezing, the cause will be either of the following:

DUST. Caused by mouldy hay, or very dusty grass in summer. If so, will soon recover. *COLDS.* Sometimes in cold or damp weather, colds become prevalent. They can also be caused by draught and badly ventilated sheds. Sneezing and a discharge from the nose is noticeable. Isolate infected stock in a warm, well-aired place. *SNUFFLES.* This is known to be the advanced stages of a cold. Frequent fits of sneezing, discharging from the nose, and continually wiping with front feet.

Damp patches are noticeable inside front feet from wiping. There is little definite knowledge regarding this complaint and scientists are of divided opinion.

It is infectious and contagious. Needs care in handling in early stages to prevent spread. Do not breed from rabbits with snuffles. The complaint does not appear to damage their health. Rabbits in badly ventilated shed are the usual sufferers, and it spreads quickly under such conditions. Very rarely noticed in outside hutches.

EAR CANKER

If a rabbit is noticed shaking its head and occasionally scratching its ear with its hind feet, examine the inside of the ear for ear canker. Ear canker is a cankerous sediment inside the base of the ear, and if not checked will completely fill up the ear. This is very painful, and sufferers lose condition. Most prevalent with the large varieties of rabbits such as Flemish Giants and Lops.

The remedy is quick and easy. Use oil which has been through the engine of a motor, known by garages as sump oil. When first noticing, soak the ear with the oil, the next day take out as much as possible of the sediment with a pointed stick, and add more oil. Avoid bleeding – if any signs of bleeding leave till the following day. The third day take out any remaining core and again add oil. When the ear is thoroughly clean, dust with flowers of sulphur. Should not recur. It is contagious, and the infected hutches should be thoroughly cleaned and disinfected.

VENT DISEASE

When rabbits are kept in very dirty condition, particularly without litter, it will sometimes be found on examination that their organ is swollen and inflamed. If rabbits so affected are mated, the disease will spread rapidly to both sexes. Apply zinc ointment daily for 10 days, when the complaint should be completely cured. Isolate and thoroughly disinfect hutch.

DIARRHOEA

The most prevalent trouble with rabbits is scours, i.e. diarrhoea. The cause is far more important than the cure, to prevent others contracting it through the same mistake. The main causes are the quality of foods and types of food used and irregular feeding. The result causes indigestion produced by gorging or inability to digest the quantity or quality of the food given. It is sometimes caused by a chill. A typical cause is not feeding rabbits at regular intervals, resulting in them getting very hungry at times, then feeding with an abundance of young succulent greenfood, when the rabbits will sit in one place and gorge, and eat far more than they are able to digest. Often the rabbit is in a bad state before it is noticed; in fact often quite beyond recovery.

Bad sufferers which cannot be tempted with choice tit-bits have no chance of recovery. As soon as signs of diarrhoea are noticed, change over to dry feeding, hay and mash in small tempting quantities. Shepherds' purse which grows wild in the garden (keep a bunch dried in reserve), blackberry and oak leaves are a good remedy. When rabbits are in advanced stages and not taken in hand soon enough, tempt them to eat even if with a small amount of cabbage leaves bringing them back to their normal appetite. Other causes are sudden change in food, frozen foods and fermented foods.

SORE EYES

Rabbits frequently get a damaged eye from fighting or by getting poked with a stiff stalk of hay or straw. Although the damage is at first slight, the natural instinct is for the rabbit to aggravate the irritation by scratching, until the damage is considerable and maybe permanent. Bathe frequently with cotton wool, soaked in a weak solution of boracic lotion. Cream is also good.

Baby rabbits are sometimes prevented from opening their eyes by the formation of a sticky gumlike discharge. This is usually first noticed at 10 to 14 days. Permanent damage may result, unless taken in hand quickly. Adopt the foregoing treatment; in stubborn cases rub with vaseline.

POT-BELLY

Extended insides, giving intense pain, usually occurs with young growing rabbits. This complaint is commonly known as pot-belly. It is usually caused by overeating greenfood when too succulent and young, and lack of exercise. In many cases it is due to irregular feeding. By overtaxing the digestive organs, and preventing the stomach juices from assimilating the rapid influx of food, gases are given off internally from the decomposition of the greenfood in the paunch. If the life of the rabbit is to be saved, action must be taken in the early stages; if allowed to remain in this condition for several hours, mortification will set in, when it is necessary to kill the rabbit to prevent further suffering. *Treatment:* Give good hay, bread and milk, to which add one teaspoonful of bicarbonate of soda. Feed in great moderation for several days after recovery; the digestive organs will be very weak for quite a time. Cures can also be effected by puncturing the swollen part with a large needle, allowing gases to escape.

CONSTIPATION

When a rabbit mopes in the hutch, with fur standing up, and droppings very hard and dry, it will usually be found to be suffering from stoppage, more generally known as constipation. The usual cause is from feeding too much dry and concentrated food, and lack of exercise. More greens or roots should be added to the diet. *Treatment:* Give a teaspoonful of medicinal paraffin; this usually suffices. Failing this, a teaspoonful of castor oil. (Amounts for adults, smaller rabbits in proportion.) Rabbits recovering from acute attacks usually finish by having diarrhoea. Discretion is therefore necessary when administering cures for the two extreme types of ailments.

SORES

Rabbits are natural fighters, the males being especially spiteful when nearing maturity. It is often found when numbers have been running together, that they have damaged each other with scratches which have developed into sores, usually in the vicinity of the rump and neck. *Treatment:* Treat affected places with zinc ointment, vaseline or fat. Recovery is usually rapid, but generally leaves the fur uneven, and takes considerable time to get prime for pelting purposes.

TREATMENT

To control complaints with rabbits, it is necessary to keep a regular observation when feeding, and the slightest irregularity is noticed in appearance or behaviour to examine carefully. It so often happens that the rabbit is beyond cure before being detected. Rabbits which have completely lost their appetite stand no chance of recovery unless they are dosed by hand. This stage is rarely reached with rabbits under the supervision of an observant operator. Hand-dosing is done by prising open the mouth with a piece of wood and holding its head back while the medicine is poured down the throat with a teaspoon. Then gently massage the throat, forcing the liquid down. The rabbit should be handled carefully for this operation. In spite of being ill it will struggle, and undue exertion may aggravate the complaint. The best method is to put the rabbit in a small box, the approximate size of the rabbit, place a sack round the rabbit's body to prevent struggling.